Courts and Doctors

Courts and Doctors

BY

LLOYD PAUL STRYKER

BeardBooks

Washington, D.C.

PREFACE

IT is axiomatic that no one is immune to lawsuits. In this regard physicians are certainly no exception. In the last twenty years it has been apparent that there has been a constant increase in New York, at least, of the number of physicians sued for malpractice. One of the important committees of the Medical Society of the State of New York, under the chairmanship of Dr. John Alling Card, has prepared some very interesting statistical data bearing upon this question. The membership of the Medical Society of the State of New York is approximately 12,500 physicians. In 1930 there were 256 more malpractice suits brought against members of the Medical Society of the State of New York than in 1929, a thirty-three per cent. increase, and representing one suit for malpractice for every twenty-two members of the Society.

The physician who is subject to a malpractice suit may be engaged in any specialty, and no group of physicians is free from the possibility of such a suit. The physicians called upon to defend themselves in court have been in practice on an average of eight years when suit was brought against them. The tremendous opportunities open to a disgruntled patient to bring an action against a physician are practically unlimited, and indicate the vital necessity for the physician to be acquainted with the present status of the law of malpractice.

The doctor is, in a measure, a quasi public servant, in that he is licensed to practice; and being licensed to practice, the State exercises certain privileges and determines in a large measure the conditions under which the physician shall practice. The doctor is relieved from jury duty and enjoys certain other privileges by reason of being a physician, and, in a large measure, has certain responsibilities to the social body. The physician contacts with the law in many and divers ways, not only through actions for his own alleged malpractice, but for the alleged negligent acts of those employed by him. He contacts with the National Prohibition Law and is constantly under the restrictions of the Federal Narcotic Law. I venture to remark that very few doctors know the substance of the National Prohibition Law or the Federal Narcotic Law, and Article 85 is practically unknown to the practicing physician.

Mr. Stryker was for many years general counsel for the Medical Society of the State of New York, and during that period had personal charge of the legal policy of the Society and the defense of its members who were sued for malpractice. Before resigning as general counsel of the Society, he was requested by its Executive Committee to put in book form the results of his experiences and his researches in the law of this subject. It was felt that his unusual knowledge and experience in this field should be preserved in permanent form, and that a book by him would constitute an authoritative discussion of the legal problems of the medical profession.   Mr. Stryker is exceptionally qualified to write this book by reason of his long experience as trial counsel and his handling for many years of medico-legal problems, both in the trial and appellate courts, as well as before committees of the legislature, and he has thus been able to bring together in this volume the material with which his personal contact with doctors and the courts has made him most familiar.

It has been a distinct pleasure for me to have read *Courts and Doctors* from beginning to end.   I am pleased that the author has been able to include so much worth-while information and to present it with such keen insight and analytical power.   The book should be not only owned, but read by every doctor as a means of informing himself as to his inherent rights and privileges, and the conditions under which he might invite a suit; and finally, for the sane advice that the author has been able to present by example and precept, whereby a physician may, in a measure, protect and fortify himself against shameless attacks upon his professional conduct, art and skill.

I believe that this volume serves a most useful purpose and I heartily recommend it to my colleagues of the medical profession.

CHAS. GORDON HEYD,

President-Elect, Medical Society
of the State of New York.

CONTENTS

CONTENTS

PART IV

DEFENSES TO ACTIONS FOR MALPRACTICE

PART V

EXPERT TESTIMONY

PART VI

THE DOCTOR ON THE WITNESS STAND

PART VII

THE DOCTOR AND THE CRIMINAL LAW

INTRODUCTION

WHEN a century hence some traveler turns his eyes upon the Place Vendome, perhaps in the place of the column fashioned from the conquered guns to perpetuate the name of Bonaparte, there will stand a higher monument to the memory of Pasteur. The era of the conqueror is passing, the day of the scientist is at hand. Mortal ears are still attuned to martial music, but there will come a time when enthusiasms higher than those born of brass and drum beat, will stir men to the march of science, and the plaudits of the multitude will reverberate, not for the victors of men, but for the conquerors of microbes, pestilence and disease. The pages of history will one day cease applauding Alexander, Caesar and Napoleon, and will lift to their proper pedestals the names of Leeuwenhoek, Spallanzani, Pasteur, Koch, Lister, Metchnikoff, David Bruce, Walter Reed, Paul Ehrlich, Banting and Noguchi.

The scientists form the first line of attack upon the enemies of the human race, but just behind them and in close contact are the practitioners of the healing art. The scientist experiments and proves, the doctor takes the discovery and applies it for the benefit of mankind. Each is dependent upon the other, both are indispensable. The history of these avocations is the story of man's rise from barbarism to the splendors of Athens and Rome, his decline through the long medieval night, his awakening with the Renaissance, and his scientific rebirth during the last hundred years.

It is a far cry from the time of Hippocrates in the early centuries of Greece, yet it is to him that we must turn not only for the ethical concept enunciated in an oath which medical men still take, but for the real beginnings of clinical medicine,—the close observation and accurate interpretations of symptoms. Then came Galen with his "healing power of nature." There followed the Alexandrian school, with Herophilus, Eristratus and their more accurate studies of anatomy. The Romans came with their scant contribution to the field of medicine, and their slavish following of Galen. With the fall of Rome, the Arabians for many centuries held the field,—from them came the first pharmacopoeia. The Renaissance followed with Paracelsus, Vesalius with the first systematic dissection of the human body, and Pare with his podalic version, and soon William Harvey was discovering the circulation of the blood, John Fothergill was laying the foundation for an understanding of diphtheria, Jenner was preventing smallpox by vaccination. Finally the nineteenth century was dawning bringing Semmelweis, the first successful enemy of puerperal fever, and Lister the father of antiseptic surgery. In the last thirty years the priceless boon of modern medicine has not only increased the happiness and longevity of mankind, but has become the veritable cornerstone of our civilization.

The history of medicine is a fascinating and dramatic story. It deserves to be better known by laymen. Professor Howard W. Haggard in his recent brilliant book with its arresting title,—"Devils, Drugs and Doctors"—has done much to interest the lay mind in the story of the healing art. His description of the incredible barbarisms that once attended childbirth, and the slow march towards the obstetrics of our day, his portrayal of the progress of surgery and his chapters on the passing of plagues and pestilence afford thrilling and authentic reading to the layman. But nowhere in his book is there a more dramatic story than the first demonstration of the use of anaesthesia.

It was October 16, 1846. The amphitheatre of the Massachusetts General Hospital was crowded. Dr. Warren, the senior surgeon of the staff was about to operate for tumor. His assistants were ready, so were the guards who were to hold the shrieking, struggling patient. All was in readiness, but still they waited. Young Dr. Thomas Green Morton, a Boston dentist and a student at the Harvard Medical School was expected. He was only twenty-eight, but he had been experimenting many years with sulphuric acid. Once when he had rendered his pet dog insensible he remarked to his wife: "The time will come, my dear, when I will banish pain from the world." When friends laughed at his experiments he said: "I shall succeed. There must be some way of deadening pain." Not only did he experiment on animals, he experimented on himself. Dr. Warren heard of him and consented to let him demonstrate his work upon a patient.

And now the amphitheatre is filled. All are waiting for young Morton,—but he does not come. Finally the senior surgeon is remarking: "As Dr. Morton has not arrived I presume he is otherwise engaged." He was about to proceed with his operation when Morton entered. It was no friendly audience that greeted him. Incredulity was written on every face. Humbug was suspected. Turning to him Dr. Warren said: "Well, sir, your patient is ready." Unperturbed by the incredulous stare of his unfriendly audience, Morton went to work. He adjusted his apparatus and promptly began the administration of the anaesthetic. Turning to the senior surgeon presently he said: "Dr. Warren, your patient is ready." And then something new occurred in the annals of surgery. The patient neither struggled nor cried out while the incision was made. The operation was continued and still no outcry. Finally the tumor was removed and still there was no sign of pain. Turning to the startled audience, slowly and emphatically Dr. Warren said: "Gentlemen, this is no humbug," and Jacob Bigelow, likewise an eye witness, observed: "I have seen something today that will go round the world." [1]

Twenty-two years later they wrote on Morton's tomb that through him "pain in surgery was averted and annulled; before whom in all times, surgery was

agony; since whom science has control of pain." [2]
And in the following year Dr. Oliver Wendell
Holmes declared before the Massachusetts Histori-
cal Society: "A little before the first half of this
century was completed, in the autumn of 1846, the
great discovery went forth from the Massachusetts
General Hospital, which repaid the debt of America
to the science of the old world, and gave immortality
to the place of its origin in the memory and the heart
of mankind. The production of temporary insensi-
bility, at will—tuto, cito, jucunde, safely, quickly,
pleasantly—is one of those triumphs over the in-
firmities of our mortal condition which changed the
aspect of life ever afterwards. Rhetoric can add
nothing to its glory; gratitude, and the pride permitted to human weakness, that our Bethlehem
should have been chosen as the birthplace of the new
embodiment of the divine mercy, are all we can yet
find room for." [3]

With such triumphs as this to its credit and count-
less scores of others since, we might expect that mankind would never tire of erecting monuments in honor
of a profession that has spent itself to make life en-
durable on this earth. It is, however, all too frequently the display of an inclination quite the oppo-
site, that is the occasion of this book. "Unfortunately in many cases," Dr. Haggard has well written,
"the attitude toward medical science is not merely
one involving a lack of enthusiasm and indifference
to benefits conferred, but is rather one of active opposition. The anti-vaccinationists, for instance, op-

pose one of the most essential and best proved measures of preventive medicine; and it is due to them that smallpox persists. The anti-vivisectionists oppose medical investigation both for the winning of new knowledge and for the application of knowledge already won. The adherents of cult-healing advocate the abolition of all medical science. Although they are a minority of the voting population, they are an active minority who take advantage of the indifference of the majority of our people. They continually introduce laws obstructing medical science and at every opportunity create difficulties for the legal maintenance of medical control. Through their activity the compulsory vaccination laws have already been repealed in two states. Unfortunately, smallpox does not respect state lines or remain where legislation favors it, but is carried into other states. The complete eradication of smallpox in the United States is thus prevented." [4]

With brilliant strokes Dr. Haggard then portrays the consequences that would ensue from the loss of modern medicine. "Let us consider," he says, "what would happen to New York or London or any other large city if it were deprived of medical science. Its civilization would go back not merely fifty years, it would go back five hundred years, if indeed, the demoralization and panic at first produced did not destroy the city entirely. The result would not be confined to such inconveniences as the loss of electricity or steam or any other products of physical science would occasion. It would be a matter of life and death for the greater part of the inhabitants of any city, large or small. The pestilences would return. Epidemics would sweep across the country and within a decade the greater part of the population would be wiped out. Even those advantages which we owe to the physical sciences and to engineering, instead of assisting in protection, would rather contribute to the spread of disease. Not only would great cities dwindle to a fraction of their present size, but in these disease-ridden towns the people would be sickly and generally short lived. Large sections of the world which are now prosperous would become uninhabitable. Yellow fever would return to Panama and would block traffic through the canal. Such facilities for travel as the railroad, the steamship and the airplane would spread disease with far greater rapidity than would the stage coach or the sailing ship. . . . Diseases now almost forgotten would return to take their place with the existing pestilences. Leprosy would again spread, for the disease has foci in the United States. Surgery would be the rough wound surgery of the ancients. Aseptic obstetrics would be replaced by the medieval midwife or the hospital with an enormous death rate from puerperal fever. Dentistry would be confined to brutal extractions without anaesthetics. It is not mere imagination, but the cold truth to say that modern civilization and the use of the inventions and discoveries of physical science would be utterly impossible were it not for medical protection." [5]

Against the general indifference of the public

toward the medical profession, it is refreshing and consoling now and again to hear a great voice honoring and extolling both the cause of medicine and its practitioners. "There are those," said Judge Cardozo in a brilliant paper read before the New York Academy of Medicine two years ago, "who say that the earliest physician was the priest, just as the earliest judge was the ruler who uttered the divine command and was king and priest combined. Modern scholarship warns us to swallow with a grain of salt these sweeping generalities, yet they have at least a core of truth. Our professions—yours and mine—medicine and law—have divided with the years, yet they were not far apart at the beginning. There hovered over each the nimbus of a tutelage that was supernatural, if not divine. To this day each retains for the other a trace of the thaumaturgic quality distinctive of its origin. The physician is still the wonder-worker, the soothsayer, to whose reading of the entrails we resort when hard beset. We may scoff at him in health, but we send for him in pain. The judge, if you fall into his clutches, is still the Themis of the Greeks, announcing mystic dooms. You may not understand his words, but their effects you can be made to feel. Each of us is thus a man of mystery to the other, a power to be propitiated in proportion to the element within it that is mystic or unknown." [6]

But great as are its triumphs of the past, Judge Cardozo shadows forth for the medical profession a future even more brilliant and infinitely larger in its scope. Speaking of the various proposals whereby administrative boards of psychiatrists and physicians should, after a jury has determined a prisoner's guilt, determine the appropriate socio-penal treatment adequate to the individual delinquent, he declares his belief "that at a day not far remote the teachings of bio-chemists and behaviorists, of psychiatrists and penologists, will transform our whole system of punishment for crime. Vain is the attempt to forecast here and now the lines of the transfigured structure. We must keep a sharp lookout, or you will supplant us altogether. . . . How it will work out, whether we shall sit beside you or above you, or even perhaps below you, I am not wise enough to say. The physician may be merely the ally of the judge in the business of admeasuring the sentence, or, as to that branch of the work, may even drive the judge away. Detention of the offender may retain in respect of certain crimes the qualities, or some of them, belonging to our present system of imprisonment, and for other crimes may acquire a quality less punitive and rigorous. But transformation there will be." [7]

Whether or not we may one day see in our whole prison system a blot upon our civilization as dark as that revealed in the English prisons and pest houses of a century and a half ago, Judge Cardozo expressed himself as certain that "whatever enlightenment shall come will make its way, not through the unaided labor of the men of my profession, the judges and the advocates, but through the combined labors of men of many callings, and most of all your own. . . .

Your hands must hold the torch that will explore the dark mystery of crime—the mystery, even darker, of the criminal himself, in all the deep recesses of thought and will and body. Here is a common ground, a border-land between your labors and our own, where hope and faith and love can do their deathless work." [8]

From another celebrated lawyer who at the time also happened to be President of the United States, have likewise come words of prophesy as to the future influence of the medical profession. Speaking before the American Medical Association in March 1927, President Coolidge said: "It is to your profession, in its broadest sense untrammelled by the contentions of different schools that the world may look for large contributions towards its regeneration physically, mentally and spiritually, when not force but reason will hold universal sway." [9]

With such a splendid heritage of past achievement and with such golden hopes for its future, it is deplorable that there are questions, many of grave import, which distract and imperil the medical profession at this time. Not the least of these is the economic problem. There is no class of men, no calling, no profession, that without thought or hope of reward, gives so lavishly of its time and strength as the medical profession. The free medical care given by doctors to the community has been estimated by Dr. Charles Gordon Heyd to represent a cash value of $365,000,000 annually. [10] "He cannot," Dr. Samuel Kopetzky has well said, "make this enormous gift to the needy and discharge his personal obligations if his economic stability is undermined by mistaken conceptions of philanthropy on the part of well-meaning, but misguided lay groups." [11]   The doctor is an individualist, as an individual he has pushed forward the frontiers of knowledge, the loss of his independence will entail an even greater loss for the public.

But it is another ill of the medical profession,—an ill having grave economic possibilities—which is the occasion of this book—an ill which is due both to a public misunderstanding of the medical profession and the unscrupulousness of certain types of patients. I refer, of course, to the increasing frequency with which doctors are being sued for malpractice.   This evil is not new.   More than half a century ago Dr. Oliver Wendell Holmes was writing that "the profession has just been startled by a verdict against a physician ruinous in its amount,—enough to drive many a hard working young practitioner out of house and home—a verdict which leads to the fear that suits for malpractice may take the place of the panel game and child stealing as a means of extorting money.   If the profession in this state, which claims a high standard of civilization, is to be crushed and ground beneath the upper millstone of the dearth of educational advantages and the lower millstone of ruinous penalties for what the ignorant ignorantly shall decide to be ignorance, all I can say is 'God save the Commonwealth of Massachusetts.' " [12]

But the hazard of a malpractice suit is far greater

now than when Dr. Holmes thus wrote. Since the enactment of workmen's compensation laws and other statutes curtailing the practice of certain lawyers, there has been a veritable flood of such cases. Especially is this true in New York State. To meet the oft expressed desire of my many friends of the medical profession for a short statement of the essential legal principles by which their work is governed, this book has been written. Its reading, it is hoped, may serve for the medical man to throw some light upon his legal rights and duties as a practitioner, and may help to prevent such part of the litigation as is preventable. And yet it should be remembered that a mere knowledge of the law is not always enough to forestall trouble, and that in any legal problem the facts are more troublesome than the law. For, as Judge Cardozo has well said: "More and more we lawyers are awaking to a perception of the truth that what divides and distracts us in the solution of a legal problem is not so much uncertainty about the law as uncertainty about the facts—the facts which generate the law. Let the facts be known as they are, and the law will sprout from the seed and turn its branches toward the light." [13]

In the writing of these pages I have entertained a larger hope than merely to set down the legal principles in which a doctor should be interested. I have hoped that by so doing the medical profession may come to a better understanding of the courts and of the problems with which judges wrestle. I have also been bold enough to hope that judges might thereby approach with even greater sympathy and understanding the difficulties of the doctor. The importance to an honorable physician, who has spent a lifetime in building a professional reputation, of a lawsuit in which his very means of livelihood are assailed, is incalculable. The duty of giving such a man a fair trial, is one of the most important which can befall a judge. It is a duty in the performance of which the judge might well recall the words of Mr. Justice Holmes: "The life of the law has not been logic; it has been experience. The felt necessities of the time, the prevalent moral and political theories, intuitions of public policy, avowed or unconscious, even the prejudices which judges share with their fellow man have had a good deal more to do than the syllogism in determining the rules by which men should be governed. The law embodies the story of the nation's development through many centuries, and it cannot be dealt with as if it contained only the axioms and corollaries of a book of mathematics." [14]

PART I

THE PRACTICE OF MEDICINE

CHAPTER I

LEGAL DEFINITION OF THE
PRACTICE OF MEDICINE

IT WOULD seem appropriate to understand here at the outset of this book precisely what is meant by the "practice of medicine." We are not concerned with what Hippocrates understood by this term, how it was regarded by Herophilus or Aristratus, what the Romans in the days of Archagathus thought about it, in what way it was considered by the Mohammedans in the days of Harun al Rashid, or how the medieval Schoolmen viewed it, but what the term now means to the legislatures and the courts of modern America.

In New York the practice of medicine has thus been clearly defined: "A person practices medicine . . . who holds himself out as being able to diagnose, treat, operate or prescribe for any human disease, pain, injury, deformity or physical condition, and who shall either offer or undertake by any means or method to diagnose, treat, operate or prescribe for any human disease, pain, injury, deformity or physical condition." [1] Substantially the same definition will be found in the laws of other states. [2] The definition embraces every form of disease, pain, injury, deformity or physical condition. The act of practicing medicine consists in holding one's self out as being able either to diagnose, treat, operate or prescribe for these conditions, and by any means or method offering or undertaking to do so.

Many years ago the Supreme Court of the United States decided that each state, in the interests of the public health, is vested with the power to legislate that no person who has not shown himself to possess the proper qualifications shall be allowed to practice medicine. "The power of the state to provide for the general welfare of its people," the Supreme Court declared, "authorizes it to prescribe all such regulations as in its judgment will secure or tend to secure them against the consequences of ignorance and incapacity as well as of deception and fraud. . . . Few professions require more careful preparation by one who seeks to enter it than that of medicine. It has to deal with all those subtle and mysterious influences upon which health and life depend, and requires not only a knowledge of the properties of vegetable and mineral substances, but of the human body in all its complicated parts, and their relation to each other, as well as their influence upon the mind. The physician must be able to detect readily the presence of disease and prescribe appropriate remedies for its removal. Everyone may have occasion to consult him, but comparatively few can judge of the qualifications of learning and skill which he possesses. Reliance must be placed upon the assurance given by his license, issued by an authority competent to judge in that respect, that he possesses the requisite qualifications. Due consideration, therefore, for the protection of society may well induce the state to exclude from practice those who have not such a license, or who are found upon examination not to be fully qualified. . . . No one has a right to practice medicine without having the necessary qualifications of learning and skill. . . ." [3]

The protection of the public health, the Supreme Court of Massachusetts has declared, "is an object of such vital importance to the welfare of the state that any rational means to that end must be upheld." [4] Exercising its power to regulate the practice of medicine it is proper for the legislature, declares the Supreme Court of California, "to protect the people from the imposition of quacks and charlatans" by prescribing "what are and what are not proper qualifications for those to possess who would engage in this calling." [5] To this end the legislatures of the various states have set up standards and have compelled those who seek to enter the profession to demonstrate, through the medium of examination, that they have complied with those standards. [6]

Having protected the public by declaring that only those who are fit to do so may engage in the practice of medicine, the legislatures have made it a criminal offense for a person who has not been licensed to hold himself out as a legal practitioner. The New York law is very specific on this subject. It says that "any person who not being then lawfully licensed or authorized to practice medicine within this state shall (a) practice or advertise to practice medicine; or (b) use in connection with his name any designation tending to imply or designate him as a practitioner of medicine; or (c) use the title 'doctor' or any abbreviation thereof in connection with his name or with any trade name in the conduct of any occupation or profession involving or pertaining to the public health or the diagnosis or treatment of any disease, pain, injury, deformity or physical condition unless duly authorized by law to use the same . . . shall be guilty of a misdemeanor . . . punishable by imprisonment for not more than one year or by a fine of not more than five hundred dollars, or by both such fine and imprisonment for each separate violation, and for a second offense shall be punishable by both such fine and imprisonment." [7]   Under the authority of this statute, it has been held that a chiropractor who diagnoses various ailments and treats the same, but who is not licensed to practice medicine, is guilty of a crime.[8]

Having thus seen that the law protects the public against the unskilled, as well as against the charlatan, we shall now observe how well, and in what way it defends the lawful practitioner in the exercise of his calling, as well as how the patient is safeguarded in his rights.

PART II

THE RELATIONSHIP OF PATIENT AND PHYSICIAN

CHAPTER II

DOCTOR AND PATIENT—THE NATURE OF THE RELATIONSHIP

THE relationship of patient and physician is to the highest possible degree a fiduciary one, involving every element of trust and confidence. The practice of medicine and surgery is a high calling. Of its practitioners the highest qualities of character are demanded. Every member of the profession upon entering it takes the Hippocratic oath to follow, according to his ability and judgment, whatever he considers for the benefit of his patients, and to abstain from whatever is deleterious or mischievous. "With purity and holiness I will pass my life and practice my art. . . . Into whatever houses I enter I will go into them for the benefit of the sick and will abstain from every voluntary act of mischief and corruption." Thus reads this ancient pledge.

The Principles of Medical Ethics and Professional Conduct of the American Medical Association and the various state societies, reaffirm the lofty ethical concepts expounded by the founder of medicine. They lay emphasis upon the fact that the practice of medicine is not a business, but a profession. "A profession has for its prime object the service it can render to humanity; reward or financial gain should be a subordinate consideration. The practice of medicine is a profession. In choosing this profession an individual assumes an obligation to conduct himself in accord with its ideals." [1]   The obligation assumed on entering the profession "requires the physician to comport himself as a gentleman and demands that he use every honorable means to uphold the dignity and honor of his vocation, to exalt its standards and to extend its sphere of usefulness." [2]   A physician should be " 'an upright man, instructed in the art of healing.' Consequently, he must keep himself pure in character and conform to a high standard of morals, and must be diligent and conscientious in his studies. 'He should also be modest, sober, patient, prompt to do his whole duty without anxiety; pious without going so far as superstition, conducting himself with propriety in his profession and in all the actions of his life.' " [3]   Thus speak the Principles of Medical Ethics of the American Medical Association. "The Medical Profession exacts from its members the highest type of character and morals, and to attain such a standard is a duty every physician owes alike to the profession and to the public. It is incumbent on physicians to be temperate in all things, for the practice of medicine requires the unremitting exercise of a clear and vigorous mind." [4]   Physicians should "not only be ever ready to respond to the calls of the sick and the injured, but should be mindful of the high character of their mission and of the responsibilities they incur in the discharge of their professional duties. In their ministrations they should

never forget that the health and the lives of those entrusted to their care depend on skill and attention." [5]
Thus speak the Principles of Professional Conduct
adopted by the Medical Society of the State of New
York. Similar principles adopted by other state societies throughout the Union demonstrate the high
ethical professional plane upon which doctors place
their calling.

How truly the profession as a whole has lived up
to its own exalted standards is one of the glories of
this high calling. Experienced in life, and men and
courts, the late Chief City Magistrate McAdoo, at
the close of his long and notable career of public
service, once remarked: "The medical profession is
among the noblest, and to me it is a sacred one. It
is in the forefront of civilization. . . . It has made
more advances in dealing with human suffering and
preventable death than all other agencies. . . . If
ever there is a roster of secular saints, the medical
profession will crowd the ranks." [6]

Whether admitting to the full the justification for
this high praise, every doctor will concede that he has
not infrequently encountered patients dealing with
whom required many of the qualities of a saint. The
doctor is a clinician not only in pathology, but in human nature. He will encounter every human trait
ranking all the way from thankfulness and appreciation to cold indifference, perversity and downright
malice. He must be prepared for whatever quality
he meets, and must be able to cope with it as he finds it.
He must, if he would attain proficiency and success,

study his men and women as painstakingly as he ponders their diseases. A genuine interest in mankind will help him to overlook many an ungracious quality, a sense of humor will act as a great solvent, the possession of tact will prove of inestimable assistance.

I never kept accurate statistics on the subject, but I always felt that not a few of the controversies between doctors and their patients coming to my notice, might have been prevented by a greater display of tact by the physician. Tact has been defined as a "fine sense of how to avoid giving offense." It has likewise been described as "fineness of discernment as to action or conduct." Others have spoken of it as an "intuitive sense of what is true, right or proper." A fine sense of anything presupposes a sense well developed,—an alert and a trained mind. A sense of how to avoid giving offense could only come from a consideration of the rights, the sensibilities, even the prejudices of others. An intuitive sense of what is true, right and proper can spring only from a generous character and sound ethical development.

Tact is a priceless asset for any professional man, it is indispensable to the physician. The ills, deformities, physical and mental states of people form the subject-matter of his life's work. He encounters all kinds of conditions of men and women, appreciative as well as critical, intelligent as well as ignorant, reasonable as well as unreasonable, fair as well as mean, generous as well as selfish. From the most unpromising of these, he may fashion warm friendships, or sometimes bitter enmities. How he will fare with his patients (granting of course reasonable competency) will largely depend upon his sense of tact or on his lack of it.

A man of fine mental perception will not be puffed up or unduly impressed with his own importance or attainments, he will not unduly struggle to impress, or indulge in pompous polysyllables. Uttering valuable advice to medical students as to their relations with their future patients, Dr. Oliver Wendell Holmes well said: "The less pretension you make, the better they will like you in the long run. . . . I know there are professors in this country who 'ligate' arteries. Other surgeons only tie them, and it stops the bleeding just as well." [7]

A man with fineness of discernment will well seek to persuade rather than command. Benjamin Franklin in his priceless autobiography, has told us how he schooled himself in the use of "terms of modest diffidence, never using when I advanced anything that may possibly be disputed, the words certainly, undoubtedly, or any others that give an air of positiveness to an opinion, but rather say, I conceive or apprehend a thing to be so and so, it appears to me, or I should think it so and so, for such and such reasons, or I imagine it to be so, or it is so if I am not mistaken. This habit, I believe, has been of great advantage to me when I have had occasion to inculcate my opinions and persuade men into measures that I have been from time to time engaged in promoting, and as the chief ends of conversation are to inform or to be informed, to please or to persuade, I wish well meaning sensible men would not lessen their power of doing good by a positive or assuming manner that seldom fails to disgust, tends to create opposition and to defeat every one of the purposes for which speech was given to us. . . ."

Tact is not a synonym for cowardice. Tact does not require a weak or indifferent acquiescence in what is wrong or untrue. Tact is the high ability of the broad-minded so to conduct themselves with their fellow men as to avoid friction, needless annoyance and unnecessary hatred. Tact involves the effort to understand another's point of view and to give it due weight and consideration. The development of tact requires the fostering of largemindedness, openmindedness and fairness. A tactful man is an understanding man, usually a large man.

The principles governing the relationship of patient and physician must be sensed and felt, rather than defined. The law has laid down only the more obvious rules. The doctor with fineness of mental perception will discern for himself the subtle character of the relationship, and the quality of its obligations. If his intuitive sense of what is true, right and proper does not lead him to avoid the more obvious pitfalls, no book can help him. Nevertheless, he should know the elementary things which the courts have said upon this subject.

CHAPTER III

THE DOCTOR'S DUTY TO HIS PATIENT

MANY a physician who has found himself cast in the unenviable rôle of defendant in a malpractice action, in one form or another, has expressed to me his hearty accord with the celebrated dictum of Charles Macklin that "the law is a sort of hocus-pocus science, that smiles in yer face while it picks yer pocket; and the glorious uncertainty of it is of mair use to the professors than the justice of it."   But as he begins to see with what understanding and justice the law prescribes his duties and defends his rights, he may,— especially after a jury has rendered a verdict in his favor—be more willing to admit that the Lord Chancellor in "Iolanthe" was not utterly mistaken when he sang:

> "The law is the true embodiment
> of Everything that's excellent."

In a manner unsurpassed for clarity and brevity, the New York Court of Appeals thirty-two years ago, in its luminous opinion in the Pike case laid down the law on this subject.   This famous decision has been quoted with approval throughout the length and breadth of the United States.   Its clear language has frequently been elaborated upon, but never improved by the courts of other jurisdictions. "A physician and surgeon, by taking charge of a case," the New York Court declared, "impliedly represents that he possesses, and the law places upon him the duty of possessing, that reasonable degree of learning and skill that is ordinarily possessed by physicians and surgeons in the locality where he practices, and which is ordinarily regarded by those conversant with the employment as necessary to qualify him to engage in the business of practicing medicine and surgery. Upon consenting to treat a patient, it becomes his duty to use reasonable care and diligence in the exercise of his skill and the application of his learning to accomplish the purpose for which he was employed. He is under the further obligation to use his best judgment in exercising his skill and applying his knowledge." [1]

As to the ordinary practitioner, that is, one not claiming to be a specialist, the court enunciated this fair principle: "The rule in relation to learning and skill does not require the surgeon to possess that extraordinary learning and skill which belong only to a few men of rare endowments, but such as is possessed by the average member of the medical profession in good standing." [2]   Then after emphasizing that every physician "is bound to keep abreast of the times," and that he may not depart from "approved methods in general use," the court continues: "The rule of reasonable care and diligence does not require the exercise of the highest possible degree of care. . . . His implied engagement with his patient does not guarantee a good result, but he promises by implication to use the skill and learning of the average physician, to exercise reasonable care and to exert his best judgment in the effort to bring about a good result." [8]

An analysis of this rule discloses three essential obligations which the law imposes upon a physician and surgeon who takes charge of a case: (1) That he must possess "that reasonable degree of learning and skill" that is "ordinarily possessed by physicians and surgeons in the locality where he practices," such as is ordinarily regarded by those conversant with the employment "as necessary to qualify him in practicing medicine and surgery." The words "reasonable" and "ordinarily" are the key words. The physician is not required to have that "extraordinary learning and skill which belong only to a few men of *rare endowments,* but such as is possessed by the *average* member of the medical profession in good standing." But it is not even to the general average of the profession which the individual must conform, it is enough if he possesses such a degree of learning and skill as is "ordinarily" possessed by the physician and surgeon *in the locality where he practices.* Nothing could be fairer than this rule. The doctor is not required to be a genius or a superman of medicine or surgery, he is merely required to possess and use "the skill and learning of the *average* physician." He is not judged by the high standards which may be attained in some unusually competent medical centre, but merely by that standard which is set him by his brethren in the community where he works.

In a Massachusetts case, for example, a physician

who practiced in a country town of about twenty-five
hundred inhabitants, was sued for malpractice because of his treatment of an injured wrist. The
court charged that "the defendant undertaking to
practice as a physician and surgeon in a town of comparatively small population was bound to possess that
skill only which physicians and surgeons of ordinary
ability and skill practicing in similar localities with
opportunities for no larger experience ordinarily possess; and he was not bound to possess that high degree
of art and skill possessed by eminent surgeons practicing in large cities and making a specialty of the
practice of surgery." [4]

In this connection, however, it should be noted that
the rule requiring a physician to possess merely such
knowledge and skill as is possessed by the average
physician in his locality is not applicable to specialists.
A specialist is one "who applies himself to the study
and practice of some particular branch of his profession." [5] A physician who holds himself out as being
specially versed in some phase of medicine is required
to possess special knowledge and skill, not merely
such knowledge and skill as the *average physician* has,
but such as is possessed by the *average specialist*. If
a specialist "possessed no greater skill in the line of
his specialty than the average physician," the Indiana
courts have said, "there would be no reason for his
employment; possessing such additional skill, it becomes his duty to give his patient the benefit of it." [6]
The reason for this rule, the court made plain in
these words: "Scientific investigation and research

have been extended and prosecuted so persistently and learnedly that the person affected by many forms of disease is of necessity compelled to seek the aid of a specialist in order to secure the results thereof. The local doctor in many instances himself suggests and selects the specialist whose learning and industry have given him a knowledge in the particular line which the general practitioner has neither time nor opportunity to acquire. . . . Being employed because of his peculiar learning and skill, it follows that his duty to the patient cannot be measured by the average skill of general practitioners." [7]

(2) The physician is "under the further obligation to use his best judgment," not his guess or hasty surmise, not his snap judgment, but his *"best judgment."* Judgment is the faculty of deciding wisely. This faculty is better developed in some than in others. Professional men usually take rank in proportion to their possession of this faculty. It is a faculty which can be strengthened and improved by exercise. But whatever degree of perfection in this faculty of the mind a physician may have attained, he must *"use"* it for the benefit of his patient. The law will not be satisfied with anything less than the use of "his *best judgment* in exercising his skill and applying his knowledge." Of what use are skill or knowledge if wise decisions are not made in their use? The law imperatively demands that the physician in applying his skill and knowledge must make the best decision and wisest decision within his power. But it is no defense for a doctor who departs from some duty

which he owes his patient,—such, for example, as his duty to follow the "approved methods in general use"—that in doing so he was using his best judgment. It does not, however, require him to have or use the best judgment which some other man might have used, it is not the best possible judgment, but *"his"* best judgment that he must bring to bear.

(3) The physician must "keep abreast of the times" and must follow the "approved methods in general use." He must know what is going on in medicine, what new discoveries have been made, what old opinions or conclusions have been discarded. Medical and scientific journals, text books, lecture courses, meetings of his county and state medical societies, conferences with especially equipped physicians, these and other means are at his disposal and he will fail to use them at his peril.

The physician, as the Pennsylvania courts perhaps needlessly point out, "deals not with insensate matter like a stone mason . . . but he has a human being to treat, a nervous system to tranquilize and a will to regulate and control." [8] Just how that human being ought to be treated is a question which varies with the advance of science. What was the proper and approved method of treatment of certain diseases at the time of George Washington would be regarded as sheer barbarism today. Some of the approved methods of today may seem equally obsolete a century hence. Amazing discoveries and advances have been made since Harvey discovered the circulation of the blood, but much remains to be discovered. "We are constantly confronted in our study and practice of medicine," Doctor Frederick Peterson has well written, "with the mass of our ignorance of the things yet to be known, and with the defects and limitations of the students of these things. Despite this, however, we are constantly wresting from nature her marvelous secrets and surprising and uplifting the world with our discoveries. . . . Compare the knowledge of cerebral localization at the time of Hippocrates and at the present day, and contemplate the shifting mass of ignorance concerning this subject during those twenty-three centuries. Think of the thousand preposterous assertions concerning the brain, the thousand absurdities current, the thousand errors promulgated, the work of the multitude of quacks, philosophers, psychologists, physicians, anatomists, physiologists during all these centuries before what seems to us now such simple truth won the acceptance of the modern world. And with regard to the things yet to be discovered in this great unseen and unknown universe about us, the same process of sifting the good from the bad evidence goes ever on in the self same way." [9]

While it is not easy for the busy practitioner to keep himself equipped with all that is transpiring in medicine, yet he will fail to do so at his peril. He must always know what the proper and approved practice is. In an obstetrical case which I once handled, the physician insisted when I was preparing for trial, that he had followed the most approved practice. From my study of similar cases I knew that his procedure was one that the profession had long since abandoned. "What authority, Doctor," I asked him, "did you rely upon?" He referred me to a well-known book upon obstetrics. "What edition have you in mind?" I next inquired. "The one I used in medical school," he answered. He had graduated in 1888! I promptly settled the case.

CHAPTER IV

THE PATIENT'S DUTY TO HIS DOCTOR

THE relationship of physician and patient imposes
duties on both parties to the arrangement.   It is not
all one-sided.   No doctor can secure satisfactory results unless with the coöperation of his patient, nor
can he be held responsible when his patient fails or
refuses to follow reasonable and proper instructions
or to conform to the prescription or course of treatment of his physician.   In such cases the patient is
guilty of contributory negligence.

In a famous New York case Judge Pryor charged
the jury: "All the obligation is not upon the physician,
but the patient also has his duties to discharge.   In
particular, the patient must obey the orders and follow the directions of his physician, and if he disobeys
such orders or neglects such directions, he cannot hold
the physician for the consequences of such disobedi-
ence or neglect.   Accordingly, I charge you that if
you find that the injury of which the plaintiff com-
plains was the effect of her carelessness or neglect
alone or was the effect of the defendant's negligence
or want of skill in combination and coöperation with
her own carelessness and neglect she cannot recover.
Her contributory negligence would defeat the action." [1]

23

A certain doctor in Massachusetts advised his patient to have an X-ray photograph made to determine whether or not there was a fracture. The patient regarded his pocketbook of more importance than his fractured bone and declined to have the X-ray made because of the expense entailed. Later he sued his doctor for malpractice, claiming an improper reduction of the fracture. "If," said the Supreme Court of Massachusetts, "such a photograph was essential in order to discover the fracture and the physician . . . advised that it be taken and the patient refused this advice the physician cannot be charged with negligence. The plaintiff cannot hold the defendant responsible for the consequence of his own want of care, nor attribute to him damages resulting from his own neglect and he cannot complain if the injury resulted from his refusal to follow the advice of the attending physician." [2] A patient, the court continued, "when he places himself in the care of a physician cannot decline to follow his advice or adopt his suggestion. . . . The patient cannot charge the physician with negligence if the patient himself refuses to carry out the directions." [3]

Where, however, the physician has advised the taking of an X-ray and the question is later litigated in court, the patient often denies that such instructions were given. To obviate an unfavorable determination of the issue of fact thus raised, the physician could protect himself in advance by securing from the patient a signed statement that he refused to have an X-ray taken, although the doctor had advised it.

This statement would be of immeasurable value to the doctor upon the trial.

Now, it sometimes happens that to follow the instructions of a doctor will result in pain. Patients have frequently been known to refuse to do what their doctors told them because it hurt. If the patient does this, however, he cannot later claim damages against his physician for injuries which may have resulted from his refusal to obey his doctor. The Pennsylvania courts upon this subject have declared: "Nothing can be more clear than that it is the duty of the patient to coöperate with his professional adviser and to conform to the necessary prescriptions, but if he will not or under pressure of pain cannot, his neglect is his own wrong or misfortune for which he has no right to hold his surgeon responsible. No man may take advantage of his own wrong or charge his misfortune to the account of another." [4]

Among the many other duties which the patient owes to his physician is that of returning for treatment as directed. It not infrequently happens that a patient will make several visits to his doctor and then stop coming, even though he has been instructed to return. In such cases if injurious consequences follow, the patient cannot hold his doctor liable; he is guilty of contributory negligence. [5]

If, however, the injury is first caused by the physician's negligence, the subsequent negligence of the patient is not a defense to the negligence of the physician. "The most which could be claimed on account of any subsequent negligence," declared the New

York Court of Appeals, "would be that it should mitigate the amount of the plaintiff's damages." [6]

So zealous is the law that the patient shall do his part as well as the physician, that in addition to the foregoing requirements, it has been held that a patient must exercise ordinary prudence, that is, such prudence as could reasonably be expected from an ordinarily prudent patient under similar circumstances. If he does not exercise such prudence, he cannot blame his doctor or recover for that which his imprudence has occasioned. [7]

The principles we have just been discussing appear obvious, perhaps almost platitudinous. Any layman, it would seem, should know of their existence by his intuitive common sense. Yet, I have seen numerous malpractice actions begun where the injury complained of was attributable solely to the patient's own neglect or refusal to obey the directions of his doctor, rather than to any negligence on the part of his professional adviser.

CHAPTER V

CONFIDENTIAL COMMUNICATIONS

No SUBJECT is of greater interest to the physician than the scope of his obligation and the nature of his duty with respect to the confidences of his patients. Inasmuch as the statutes vary in the different states and in some there are no statutes at all upon this subject, we have selected the New York statutes and decisions as a basis for this chapter. They are typical of the states where such laws exist.

One hundred years ago, in 1828, the New York Legislature enacted its first law protecting privileged communications made by a patient to his physician. This statute has ever since been in effect in New York State. In its present form it reads: "A person duly authorized to practice physic or surgery, or a professional or registered nurse, shall not be allowed to disclose any information which he acquired in attending a patient in a professional capacity, and which was necessary to enable him to act in that capacity; unless where the patient is a child under the age of sixteen, the information so acquired indicates that the patient has been the witness or subject of a crime, in which case the physician or nurses may be required to testify fully in relation thereto upon any examination, trial or other proceeding in which the commission of such crime is a subject of inquiry." [1]

This law the New York Court of Appeals has said, is "very explicit in forbidding a physician from disclosing any information received by him which is necessary to enable him to prescribe for a patient under his charge. It is a just and useful enactment, introduced to give protection to those who were in charge of physicians from the secrets disclosed to enable them properly to prescribe for diseases of the patient. To open the door to the disclosure of secrets revealed on the sick bed, or when consulting a physician, would destroy confidence between the physician and the patient, and, it is easy to see, might tend very much to prevent the advantages and benefits which flow from this confidential relationship. The point made that there was no evidence that the information asked for was essential to enable the physician to prescribe is not well taken, as it must be assumed from the relationship existing that the information would not have been imparted except for the purpose of aiding the physician in prescribing for the patient. Aside, however, from this, the statute in question, being remedial, should receive a liberal interpretation, and not be restricted by any technical rule. When it speaks of information, it means not only communications received from the lips of the patient, but such knowledge as may be acquired from the patient himself, from the statement of others who may surround him at the time, or from observation of his appearance and symptoms. Even if the patient could not speak, or his mental powers were so affected that he could not accurately state the nature of his disease, the astute medical observer would readily comprehend his condition.   Information thus acquired is clearly within the scope and meaning of the statute." [2]

An analysis of the statute reveals (a) that the privilege extends to duly licensed physicians or professional or registered nurses; (b) the facts thus privileged consist of "any information" which the physician or nurse acquired in attending a patient in a professional capacity, and *which was necessary to enable him to act in that capacity;* (c) the rule is mandatory, it does not authorize the physician to elect whether or not he will disclose such a confidential communication, the statute says that he *"shall not* be allowed to disclose" it.   No statute, however, can be understood without reading it in connection with the interpretations which the courts have given it.   We have seen that the relationship of patient and physician must exist.   Thus, in the Griffiths case, which was an action for negligence wherein the defendant was sued for running over a boy, a doctor who was in the employ of the defendant and who visited the boy in the hospital to ascertain the extent of his injuries, but not for the purpose of treating him, was held competent to testify to conversations with the boy, on the ground that he was not the boy's physician; the relationship of patient and physician did not exist between them. [3]

Similarly in a criminal action it was held that a

physician who examined the prisoner at the request of the District Attorney for the purpose of giving evidence as to the prisoner's sanity, was competent to testify to any information gained as a result of that examination, as the relationship of physician and patient was not there.[4]

In the Kelly case, a civil action, the plaintiff called upon the physician a few days before the trial to ascertain what testimony the physician would give. He did not call for the purpose of obtaining medical treatment. It was held that the physician should be permitted to testify at the trial as to what the plaintiff had said to him on that visit, for the reason that the relationship of physician and patient did not exist between them; that the information which he had gained was not in the course of giving professional advice or treatment.[5]

I have frequently been asked by doctors as to whether or not the fact that no fee was paid was determinative of the existence of the relationship of patient and physician and hence, of the professional privilege. This question was squarely decided in the Bauch case, where it was held that the payment of a fee was not essential to the relationship of physician and patient, and that a free patient was entitled to just as full and complete protection under the statute as a patient who had paid a fee.[6]

It is unimportant whether the physician was called by the patient himself or by a member of the patient's family or, indeed, whether he was brought in by another doctor. Even if the physician is called by an utter stranger, if he attends the patient for the purpose of giving professional advice and aid, the relationship of physician and patient exists and the privilege arises. Indeed, the fact that the patient was unconscious when the physician arrived and was unaware of the physician's presence, makes no difference. If the physician in such case attends for the purpose of giving professional attention or advice, the relationship of physician and patient is then present and the privilege is intact.[7] Thus, in Meyer vs. Knights of Pythias, it developed that the physician was summoned by a bellboy in a hotel to attend a guest who had attempted suicide by eating "Rough on Rats." It was held that the physician in that case could not divulge any information which he obtained while treating the patient.[8]

We have seen that the statute prohibits the physician from disclosing information which he acquired "in attending a patient in a professional capacity, and *which was necessary to enable him to act in that capacity.*" In the Green case an ambulance surgeon learned from bystanders as to how the accident had happened. He was permitted to testify concerning this information, since the information thus acquired was not necessary "to enable him to act" in his professional capacity.[9]

Where, however, the physician secures information from the patient which is a necessary incident of the investigations which he makes in order to treat his patient, what he learns cannot be divulged. Thus, in the Nelson case a physician while attending his patient at childbirth learned that she had an umbilical hernia.   He did not treat her for this and the knowledge of its existence was of no aid to him in caring for his patient, but his knowledge of the umbilical hernia was acquired from his patient while acting in the capacity of physician.   The court held that the physician could not testify concerning his discovery of the hernia.[10]

So, too, in the Sparer case, it appeared that an applicant for life insurance had stated in his application that he had not received medical or surgical attention within the past five years.   A doctor was called to prove that the insured had not only been treated by a surgeon, but had had an operation performed.   The doctor was not permitted to prove the insured's condition at the time of the operation, but it was held that it would have been proper to establish by the records of the hospital the fact that an operation had been performed even though the doctor who performed it could not describe the operation or any condition that he observed which was necessarily disclosed by an inspection of the body of the insured.[11]

It is only the information which the physician acquires while he is attending his patient in a *professional capacity* that he is forbidden to divulge.   The burden of proof that such information was obtained in this way rests upon the person who asserts it.[12]   Thus, in the Burley case a physician who attended a testator during the last year of his life was asked whether he observed the testator during this time *when he was not attending him as a physician.* The court held that it was competent for him to answer such questions as to the physical facts that were seen by him when he was not in attendance as a physician.[13] As to whether or not the information which the physician has gained was in fact necessary to enable him to treat the patient is a question upon which the physician himself is competent to testify.[14]

The cases on the subject of confidential communications are almost infinite in number. Among others the following communications have been held to fall within the rule of privilege. Information obtained by a physician with respect to the health of an assured while he was attending such assured as a physician;[15] the fact that a patient had a venereal disease while under a physician's care;[16] in an action for divorce, a physician was forbidden to testify as to conversations had with him by one of the parties tending to establish adultery.[17] The rule, however, does not forbid a physician from testifying that a certain person was his patient, that he attended such person as a physician, and the dates and number of times hourly or daily that he so attended such patient.[18]

Who may claim the privilege? The answer is that whenever it appears that the privilege is asserted to protect the feelings or the reputation of a living patient or the memory of one who has since died, the testimony of the physician will not be received where the objection is taken by the patient, his personal representative or a third person. Even the assignee of a cause of action may claim the privilege.[19]

In one New York case it was held that even though no objection had been taken to the testimony of a physician, the court itself is in duty bound on its own initiative to refuse to receive the testimony.[20]   In that case, however, it appeared that the patient was not present in court to object or cause his counsel to object to the testimony.   The opinion suggests that if the patient had been present in court and had heard the testimony without objection, that this would have constituted a waiver by him of the privilege in his behalf.[21]

The question of the waiver privilege has been much discussed by the courts.   This branch of the subject may be divided into three divisions: (a) actions brought by plaintiffs to recover damages for personal injuries; (b) all other civil actions; and (c) criminal prosecutions.

(a) "Where," said the Court of Appeals, "the plaintiff in an action brought to recover damages for personal injuries caused by the negligence of the defendant describes these injuries and their results and it appears that he has consulted or been treated by a physician in regard to them he waives the protection of section 834 of the Code (now section 352, Civil Practice Act).   The physician may then be called by the defendant and examined as to any information acquired by him in the course of such consultation or treatment.   The rule as it was formerly understood was altered by our decision in Capron v. Douglass (193 N. Y. 11).   We there took the position that where the patient tenders to the jury the issue as to his physical condition it must in fairness and justice be held that he has himself waived the obligation of secrecy which would otherwise exist." [22]

In the Capron case, to which the court referred, the plaintiff brought an action against a physician for malpractice in the treatment of a fracture of the tibia and fibula. One of the physicians who subsequently treated the plaintiff's leg was offered as a witness for the defendant, but was not permitted to testify on the ground that it would constitute the divulgence of a confidential communication. This objection was sustained by the trial court, but was overruled by the Court of Appeals where Judge Haight, in referring to the plaintiff's conduct, said: "He has thus permitted the condition of his broken limb to be given to the public in an open trial, thereby forever preventing it and its condition from being a secret between himself and his physician. The intent of the legislature in enacting the statute making such information privileged was, doubtless, to inspire confidence between the patient and his physician, so that the former could fully disclose to the latter all the particulars of his ailment without fear that he may be exposed to civil or criminal prosecution, or shame and disgrace, by the disclosure thus made, and thus enable the latter to prescribe for and advise the former most advantageously. . . . This action, as we have seen, was for malpractice. The plaintiff both in his complaint and in his testimony has fully disclosed all of the details of his affliction as it existed both at his home and at the hospital. He has given in much detail how the fractures occurred, how they were treated, his pain and suffering, and so far as he was able to comprehend, when not under the influence of anaesthetics, the particulars of the operation at the hospital. He, himself, has, therefore, given to the public the full details of his case, thereby disclosing the secrets which the statute was designed to protect, thus removing it from the operation of the statute. . . . The character of the action necessarily calls for a disclosure of his condition and the treatment that was adopted by the defendant and those assisting him. To hold that the plaintiff may waive the privilege as to himself and his own physicians and then invoke it as to the defendant and his physicians, would have the effect of converting the statute into both a sword and a shield. It would permit him to prosecute with the sword and then shield himself from the defense by the exclusion of the defendant's testimony. It would enable the plaintiff to testify to whatever he pleased with reference to his condition and the treatment adopted by the defendant without fear of contradiction. The plaintiff could thus establish his cause of action, and the defendant would be deprived of the power to interpose his defense by reason of the closing of the mouth of his witnesses by the provisions of the Code referred to. Such a construction of its provisions we think was never contemplated by the legislature. It would lead to unreasonable and unjust results." [23]

In this connection, I should call attention to certain provisions of another section of the Civil Practice Act (section 354) which provides that the privilege cannot be waived unless it is "expressly waived on such trial or examination by the . . . patient" or, in the case of the validity of the last will and testament of a deceased patient the privilege may be waived by the "executor or executors named in said will, or by the surviving husband, widow or any heir-at-law or any of the next of kin of such deceased, or any other party in interest." The statute further provides: "The waivers herein provided for must be made in open court on the trial of the action or proceeding, and a paper executed by a party prior to the trial providing for such waiver shall be insufficient as such a waiver. But the attorneys for the respective parties, prior to the trial, may stipulate for such waiver, and the same shall be sufficient therefor."

In the Capron case previously referred to, this section was construed and it was held that inasmuch as the plaintiff both in his complaint and his testimony had fully disclosed the details of his affliction, that he had "therefore given to the public the full details of his case, thereby disclosed the secrets which the statute was designed to protect, thus removing it from the operation of the statute." [24]

In another case in the New York Court of Appeals, it was declared: "After its publication no further injury can be inflicted upon the rights and interests, which the statute was intended to protect, and there is no further reason for its enforcement. The nature of the information is of such a character that when it is once divulged in legal proceedings, it cannot be again hidden or concealed.   It is then open to the consideration of the entire public, and the privilege of forbidding its repetition is not conferred by the statute.   The consent having been once given and acted upon cannot be recalled, and the patient can never be restored to the condition which the statute, from motives of public policy, has sought to protect." [25]

But where the patient has died, the right of the executors, administrators or representatives of the deceased is not as broad in the matter of waiving the privilege as is that of a living person.   In section 354 previously referred to, it is expressly provided that a physician may not disclose "confidential communications and such facts as would tend to disgrace the memory of the patient" where such patient has died, even though the privilege has been expressly waived by the personal representatives of the deceased. The salutary rule is thereby enacted, which prevents the disclosure of either confidential communications or facts which would disgrace the memory of the dead.   Neither the executor, administrator, next of kin nor other representatives of the deceased are competent to make a waiver which would permit such a disclosure.   Thus, in the Mulligan case, the defendant was sued as the executor of one Mary Sinski who in her lifetime had executed a promissory note. The defense interposed was that the deceased had suffered from delirium tremens and hence, was incompetent to make the note.   The defendant executor called as a witness a physician who treated the deceased prior to her death.   On his direct examination the physician was asked as to the examination of the deceased and the treatment which he had accorded her, as well as her mental condition, what she died of and whether she was rational or irrational.   Objection to these questions was sustained and this ruling was affirmed by the Appellate Division, which declared: "The power of a personal representative of a deceased patient is not as broad as that of the patient himself.   The latter's power to waive the prohibition of the statute is unlimited.   The former is forbidden, among other things, to waive the disclosure of information which would 'disgrace the memory of the patient.'   It would certainly tend to disgrace the memory of the dead to be permitted to prove that at the time of the making of an alleged contract the deceased was mentally incompetent to make the same by reason of the existence of a disease known as delirium tremens, caused by the excessive use of intoxicating liquors and alcoholic drinks." [26]

In times past this question frequently was presented to me: Where patient A has sued doctor B and has been subsequently treated by doctor C, is it permissible for doctor C (prior to the trial) to divulge the information gained by him in the treatment of the same injury without the permission of patient A?   In my judgment doctor C is fully within his rights in divulging such information.   Where the patient in his complaint has disclosed in whole or in part the facts of his condition, from the moment of the service of that complaint the privilege is waived.

In the Capron case, where it will be recalled the privilege was deemed waived, the court said: "The plaintiff both *in his complaint* and in his testimony has fully disclosed all of the details of his affliction as it existed both at his home and at the hospital." [27]   In another New York case the court said: "By bringing an action against his regular physician, who had been treating him for a disease, claiming that the subsequent treatment was malpractice, the plaintiff waived the professional privilege and the defendant was permitted to show any facts he knew bearing upon the present condition of the plaintiff." [28]   In my judgment, therefore, not only may doctor C, if called as a witness for doctor B, testify to any facts learned by him in the course of his treatment, but he may divulge such information either to doctor B or to doctor B's lawyer in advance of the trial in order to enable doctor B to prepare for trial, providing, of course, that the patient is *compos mentis* and is living.   Where the patient has died, the doctor would not be allowed to divulge such information if the information consisted either of confidential communications or facts which would tend to disgrace the memory of the patient.

(b) In actions other than for malpractice, personal injuries or the like, the privilege is not waived unless it is expressly waived in open court by the party claiming such privilege, or by the stipulation of his attorney prior to the trial.

(c) In criminal prosecutions, it has been repeatedly held that the patient's privilege cannot be used to shield a murderer or other criminal.   Thus, in the

Pierson case, where a defendant was charged with committing murder by arsenical poisoning, the testimony of the physician who had been called to attend the victim of the crime was offered by the prosecution to prove the cause of death. The Court of Appeals held that the objection to this testimony was properly overruled on the ground that the purpose of the statute was "to enable a patient to make known his condition to his physician without the danger of any disclosure by him which would annoy the feelings, damage the character, or impair the standing of the patient while living, or disgrace his memory when dead," and that the statute was not enacted for the purpose of constructing a shield for the benefit of murderers.[29] Generally stated, the law is that where the death of a patient is the subject of a criminal prosecution, the testimony of the physician who treated the deceased will not be excluded on the ground of privilege.[30]

At common law, communications made by patient to physician for the purpose of receiving medical treatment were not privileged, no matter with what confidence they were made.[31] This rule, Professor Wigmore says, "would probably have been acknowledged as a common law principle in every American court, but in New York in 1828 came a statutory innovation establishing the privilege, and the legislation of other States, accepting in this respect as in so many others the model established by the distinguished leaders of legal reform in that epoch-making movement in New York, embodied the privilege in other

statutes.   Missouri followed next in 1835; until at
the present day in one-half of our jurisdictions the
privilege is a settled part of the law." [32]

As applied and construed by the New York courts,
this professional privilege is unquestionably a reflec-
tion of sound public policy.   It permits a patient to
speak freely and openly to his doctor, so that he may
be properly treated.   On the other hand, it does not
seal the lips of the physician if there is a question of
crime involved, nor does it seal the physician's lips
where the patient later seeks to sue the doctor in
whom he has confided or some other doctor concerning the malady which was the subject of his confidential communication.   The statute is a shield and not
a sword.

While in an action for professional services the
physician may be rendered incompetent to testify to
the nature of services by reason of statutes pro-
hibiting the disclosure of confidential communications, he may,—in New York at least—nevertheless
testify as to the reasonable value of his services even
though there is nothing in the record to show the
nature of such services. [33]

PART III

THE ACTION FOR MALPRACTICE

CHAPTER VI

THE ELEMENTS OF THE ACTION

Having considered the rights and duties of the patient and of his physician, we are now in a better position to understand the nature of an action for malpractice.

The relation of patient and physician rests upon a contract, express or implied,—it is almost always implied rather than expressed. This contract raises up certain duties, a breach of one or more of which, if it leads to a bad result, is the basis of an action for malpractice. Lawyers speak of it as an action in tort sounding in contract. A tort is a civil wrong founded upon some breach of duty, this duty may arise from contract or it may be one which the law imposes. Thus, every driver of an automobile owes to every pedestrian and to every other driver on the road the duty to use due care, that is, such care as is necessary, having regard to all the surrounding circumstances, such as the time of day, the width and character of the road, whether it is wet or dry, the state of the traffic and so on. A failure to use due care resulting in injury to another is called negligence, and gives rise to an action for damages. Negligence is one of the most important branches of the law of torts. An action for malpractice is an action in negligence. It

is based upon a physician's alleged failure to comply
with the duty which the law raises up from his contract of employment.   Malpractice has been defined
as "the negligent performance by a physician or surgeon of the duties which are devolved upon him by
virtue of his contractual relations with his patient;
bad or unskillful practice by a physician or surgeon
whereby the patient is injured." [1]   Malpractice may
be the result of ignorance or wilfulness or of negligence.[2]

A plaintiff in a malpractice action as in other civil
actions must establish his case by a fair preponderance
of evidence.[3]   Now, what is it that a plaintiff must
establish?   He must prove (a) that the relationship
of patient and physician in fact existed; (b) that the
physician departed from some duty owed by him to
the patient; and (c) that that departure from that
duty was the competent producing cause of the injury
or bad result complained of.   If the plaintiff fails to
establish all or any of these elements he cannot recover.   Let us now give these elements a somewhat
more minute examination.

(a) The relationship of physician and patient must
exist.   A doctor, like any other citizen, is a free
agent.   He may accept or reject such employment as
he chooses.   He is not an inn keeper or a common
carrier.   As previously stated a physician's duty to
his patient arises out of his contract of employment,
it is measured and defined by that contract.   What is
a contract of employment?   It is an agreement
whereby a physician, at the instance and request of a

patient, agrees to diagnose, treat, operate or prescribe for that patient.   The agreement need not be
formal in its terms, it practically never is.   No form
of words or writing is required.   Any conduct by the
parties indicating an accord that one shall become the
patient of the other is sufficient.   The largeness or
smallness of the fee agreed upon (if one is agreed
upon), is immaterial, nor does it matter if anything
is said about the fee at all.   Usually nothing is said
about it, and the physician is relegated (if he is not
voluntarily paid) to his legal right to recover what
may be reasonable under the circumstances.   But if
it is understood that no fee is to be paid at all, the
doctor's obligation is no less great.   It is one of the
great glories of the medical profession that its members devote a large proportion of their time in ren-
dering their services to charity patients free of charge.
In doing so, however, the doctor assumes no less risk
and no smaller obligation than as though the services
were performed for a captain of industry.   Thus, in
a New York case the judge charged the jury that the
mere fact that the plaintiff was a charity patient in
no wise qualified the liability of the defendant doctor.[4]
In still another case a surgeon operating in a dispensary inflicted an injury on the plaintiff's hand by
cutting through a bandage to the hand itself.   The
doctor admitted that before cutting he made no examination to ascertain where the hand was or what
was concealed under the point where he applied the
shears.   In affirming a judgment of negligence
against him, the court said: "The hurried work in a

public dispensary does not excuse the lack of ordinary care. The defendant could not assume that the hand was in a safe condition and rely on it when he readily could have ascertained the condition before applying the shears." [5]

Having considered the necessity for the existence of the relationship of patient and physician, let us take up the second element in an action for malpractice:

(b) That the doctor departed from some duty which he owed his patient. We have seen that the actual contract between the patient and physician is usually most informal. What is not said, however, the law supplies. A physician usually makes no actual representation as to his ability or skill, yet "by taking charge of a case he impliedly represents that he possesses and the law places upon him the duty of possessing, that reasonable degree of learning and skill that is ordinarily possessed" by physicians of his locality.[6] Not only must he possess that skill, but "upon consenting to treat a patient it becomes his duty to use" it.[7] He must not depart from "approved methods in general use."[8] He must "keep abreast of the times," or as the Pennsylvania courts have said, he "is bound to be up to the improvements of the day."[9] Not to have or use the required skill and learning, not to use his best judgment, not to keep abreast of the times, to depart "from approved methods in general use" is a breach of duty. This breach of duty is the second element in an action for malpractice which, in order to recover, a plaintiff must establish by a fair preponderance of evidence.

It should be noted, however, that a plaintiff cannot succeed merely by establishing that the doctor was guilty of an error of judgment. "The rule requiring him to use his best judgment," said the New York Court of Appeals, "does not hold him liable for a mere error of judgment, provided he does what he thinks is best after careful examination." [10]   Thus, it may transpire that in a given case there are several different approved methods of treating a fracture or other injury or condition.   Perhaps one method may be preferable to another.   The doctor must decide, that is, he must use his best judgment as to which method he will follow.   If he errs in this he is not liable, provided he has done what he thinks is best after careful examination.   A doctor is not a guarantor or warrantor of cures.   A doctor may not, however, adopt a procedure which has been universally condemned or one which has not yet received the sanction of scientific men, and then claim that doing what he did involved a mere "error of judgment."   There is, of course, a domain beyond which he may not use his judgment.   No doctor, for example, would be heard to say that his failure to use modern asceptic precautions, where it was possible to use them, was a mere error of judgment.

Let us now consider the third and most important element in an action for malpractice:

(c) That the departure from the duty is the competent producing cause of the injury complained of.

The law of negligence is predicated upon both duty and responsibility. To hold another liable in damages, it must be shown that that other is responsible, that is, that he has caused the injury for which damages are sought as compensation. There must be a causal connection between the injury and some act or omission of the person sued.[11] A mere breach of duty alone is not sufficient. There must be a distinct and clear chain of causation between that breach and the injury for which damages are asked. Thus, there might be a breach of duty and there might be an injury, yet this would not prove a case,—there must be a causal connection between the two. The breach of duty must produce the injury; the injury must proceed from the breach of duty. "Mere lack of skill or negligence, not *causing* injury," declared Judge Taft in a celebrated case, "gives no right of action and no right to recover even nominal damages." [12]

This rule has been nowhere better expressed than in the New York case of Smith vs. Dumont, where the General Term said: "In order to entitle plaintiff to recover for the permanent injury which it was proved he had sustained, it was necessary to prove that this permanent injury *would not have been present had not the defendant been guilty of negligence or want of skill.*" [13] There must be a direct not a remote, an actual not a speculative causal connection between the breach of duty and the bad result. The case last cited was one brought against a physician for his alleged negligent treatment of a Pott's fracture.

The court declared that a "recovery will not be allowed unless the evidence shows that the injuries are a natural and probable consequence of the wrongful act or omission of the defendant. Where they are remote or speculative, the law will not enter upon an inquiry for the reason that such a degree of certainty cannot be arrived at in respect thereto as will constitute a safeguard for judicial action." [14]   Thus, in the Pike case it was said that a departure from "approved methods in general use if *it* injures the patient will render him (the physician) liable however good his intentions may have been."   And still further that "to render a physician and surgeon liable, it is not enough that there has been a less degree of care than some other medical man might have shown, or less than even he himself might have bestowed, but there must be a want of ordinary and reasonable care *leading* to a bad result." [15]

We have discussed the duties owed by a physician to his patient, the breach of which gives rise to an action for malpractice. In the trial of hundreds of such cases, I have found that it is an alleged breach of one or both of the following duties, which is the basis of the action. These two are: (a) the doctor's duty to "use reasonable care and diligence" in his professional work, and (b) his duty not to depart "from approved methods in general use" or, as it is usually stated in the trial courts, not to depart from the "proper and approved practice."   As every doctor admitted to practice medicine is presumed to possess the knowledge and skill of the average physician,[16] a plaintiff who sets out to prove the contrary will be confronted at the outset with this presumption, which would have to be rebutted by affirmative evidence.   I have never seen it established that a doctor did not possess the requisite skill or that he did not "use his best judgment."   I have never seen this done, probably for the reason that it is much easier to prove that a physician failed to employ reasonable care and diligence in that he did not follow the proper and approved practice.   What his best judgment was and whether he used it, what his knowledge and skill actually were would be difficult to establish by any proof.

CHAPTER VII

EXPERT TESTIMONY NECESSARY—RES IPSA LOQUITUR NOT APPLICABLE

NINE-TENTHS of the malpractice dramas staged in the courts centre around this theme: Was the proper and approved practice followed, and if not, did the failure to follow it cause the injury complained of? Now, who knows what the proper and approved practice was? Who can tell whether it was followed? Who can say whether a departure from the approved methods, if there was such a departure, was the cause of the injury? Neither judges nor juries of their own knowledge are competent to decide these difficult questions without the assistance of some expert guidance. They involve questions of science which can be answered by those only possessing scientific knowledge. "Negligence on the part of a physician," said the highest court of California, "consists in his doing something which he should not have done or in omitting to do something which he should have done. . . . The authorities are practically uniform in holding . . . that as to what is or is not proper practice in examination and treatment or the usual practice and treatment is a question for experts and can only be established by their testimony." [1] This rule in various forms is set forth in every well-considered American opinion dealing with this subject.[2] The wisdom of the rule was recognized by one of the wisest men of all times centuries before America was even dreamed of.   In his *Politics,* Aristotle wrote: "As the physician *ought to be judged by the physician,* so ought men to be judged by their peers. . . ."[3]

It is fortunate for the physician that "his implied engagement with his patient does not guarantee a good result."[4]   It would not do, the courts of Indiana have declared, to hold "that every physician who administers a dose of medicine, and every surgeon who performs an operation does so at his peril if the result happens to be not good; that a jury of laymen might mulct him in damages if they as laymen should think that he had been negligent in the matter complained of although his conduct has been in harmony with well-recognized, standard methods, used by physicians generally in such cases."[5]   The mere fact that there has been a bad result, said the Supreme Court of Illinois, "is of itself no evidence of negligence or lack of skill."[6]

The rule, however, that a physician does not guarantee a good result, and is not liable for the mere fact that there has been a bad one, would be of scant benefit to him were it not for the additional requirement that in order to make out a *prima facie* case the plaintiff must adduce expert testimony establishing that the physician has either lacked the necessary skill, has failed to use it or has not followed the "approved methods in general use," and that by reason thereof the injury complained of was occasioned.   No physi-

cian is ever sued when there has been a good result,
it is a bad result which gives rise to an action for malpractice.   Quite naturally a jury sympathizes with
suffering or deformity.   Swayed by this commend-
able sympathy, if twelve laymen were allowed to decide (unenlightened by expert testimony) as to the
question of skill or the propriety of the treatment and
their relation to the end result, it is safe to say that
more verdicts would be rendered against physicians
than is now the case, and most of them would be unjust.   Regardless of the care with which the court
might charge, human sympathy would culminate in
injustice.   Hence, the law declares that a *prima facie*
case is not made out, that is, that the jury will not be
given an opportunity to pass upon it, unless there is
expert testimony establishing the essential elements
of the case, i.e., that there has been a want of skill,
a failure to follow approved methods in general use
and that both or either of them have caused the injury.

Thus, in a Minnesota case, the plaintiff's tibia and
fibula of the right leg were fractured at the junction
of the lower and middle third.   Union was slow and
the defendant doctor ordered rebreaking and resetting.   He did this, but the operation was not successful.   Ulcers developed and the ankle became rigid.
"This," said the court, "is a case where a jury could
not determine the issue of defendant's negligence
without testimony from medical experts. . . .
Whether this was caused by defendant's unskillful or
negligent operation or treatment must necessarily

rest upon competent medical testimony. Bad results alone will not justify an inference of improper treatment. The skill and care of the most competent and painstaking surgeon often fails to cure or relieve. The inherent recuperative or healing powers of patients differ greatly. And even in the same person such powers may vary from time to time." [7]

In Pennsylvania, a few years ago a man's leg was crushed. A doctor was called. He rendered first-aid and after washing and dressing the wound bandaged the leg. A few hours later the patient died from loss of blood. The doctor was sued for malpractice by the wife of the deceased who claimed that a tourniquet should have been applied. She attempted to substantiate her contention by testifying that a tourniquet was an instrument in common use by medical men. "But," said the court dismissing her complaint, "there was no evidence at all from any witness competent to express an opinion that a tourniquet should have been used or that the tight bandage applied by the defendant was not fully equivalent, in short that there was any negligence shown. The jury could only have made an uninformed guess. Negligence cannot be found that way." [8]

We have previously stated that improper practice must be the cause of a bad result if the physician is to be rendered liable. The improper practice and its causal relation to the injury complained of must both be established by expert testimony. This rule was clearly illustrated in a well-considered case in Illinois. A physician there treated the plaintiff's injured finger.

Subsequently infection developed. She sued the doctor. At the trial she called physicians who testified as experts that while the defendant's treatment of the wound was proper, he had not properly sterilized his instruments. But there was no expert testimony establishing a causal relation between the improper sterilization and the subsequent bad result. That vital link in the proof was left therefore as "a matter of mere conjecture or possibility before the jury." Declaring for this reason that the plaintiff's case had not been established, the court observed: "The law seems to be well settled that the mere fact that a good result is not obtained in the cure of a wound is of itself no evidence of negligence or lack of care, but there must be affirmative proof of such negligence or lack of care and that the injuries complained of resulted therefrom. It seems also to be settled by the authorities that such proof can only be established by the testimony of experts skilled in the medical and surgical profession. . . . This evidence must, from the very nature of the case, come from experts as other witnesses are not competent to give it, nor are juries supposed to be conversant with what is peculiar with the science and practice of the profession of medicine and surgery." [9]

The New York courts have given us two able opinions on this subject. "The right of the plaintiff to recover," said the Appellate Division of the First Department, "must necessarily depend upon medical evidence, for the question is to what extent, if any, the failure of the defendants to properly treat the plaintiff aggravated the disease from which he was suffering or increased his pain or suffering. That question can be decided neither on the testimony of laymen nor by the jurors on their own knowledge and experience without testimony." [10]

In the case of Robbins vs. Nathan, the defendant was a dentist, but the same rules were held applicable. "It is true," the court there said, "that the plaintiff was ill afterward and that illness may have been attributable to the extraction of this tooth, but that does not warrant holding the defendant liable, as he does not, under the law, guarantee the result. . . . If the treatment of the defendant was unskillful or negligent, it was incumbent upon the plaintiff to show it by those qualified to testify to the proper method of performing such an operation; and if the untoward results present here might have been avoided by due care, the duty of showing that was also on the plaintiff." [11]

I remember a case I tried in which the plaintiff's intestate had developed peritonitis and had died following a Caesarean operation. The husband of the deceased sued the doctor claiming that it was negligence for him to have performed the Caesarean operation. At the trial the plaintiff called no expert witness. He did, however, call the defendant as his own witness. The defendant testified that the deceased had come to him when she was six months pregnant, had given him a history of a previous difficult birth, at which time she had been torn by instruments and the baby had died. At the time of his examination the doctor found that she had a moderately contracted pelvis. The plaintiff having furnished no expert testimony the complaint was dismissed. This is but one instance among scores of others where judges have enforced the rules which we have been here considering.

I have noticed that trial judges always pay particular respect to the famous decision of Judge Taft in the case of Ewing vs. Goode. Judge Taft at that time was sitting as an United States Circuit Court Judge of Ohio. In the Ewing case the plaintiff who was suffering from a cataract of her right eye consulted a physician specializing in eye diseases. Subsequently she developed glaucoma and her physician operated for the relief of this condition. The sight of her right eye was lost, and the vision of the left eye then became impaired. She sued her doctor for malpractice, and offered no expert testimony to establish that the doctor's negligence did in fact cause the injury. She claimed that the facts spoke for themselves,— *res ipsa loquitur*. In directing a verdict in favor of the physician, Judge Taft said: "Before the plaintiff can recover she must show by affirmative evidence— first, that defendant was unskillful or negligent and second, that his want of skill or care caused injury to the plaintiff. If either element is lacking in her proof she has presented no case for the consideration of the jury. The naked facts that defendant performed an operation on her eye, and that pain followed, and that subsequently the eye was in such bad condition that it had to be extracted, establish neither the neglect and unskillfulness of the treatment, nor the causal connection between it and the unfortunate event.   A physician is not a warrantor of cures.   If the maxim, *res ipsa loquitur* were applicable to a case like this and a failure to cure were held to be evidence, however slight, of negligence on the part of the physician or surgeon causing the bad result, few could be courageous enough to practice the healing art, for they would have to assume financial liability for nearly all the ills that flesh is heir to." [12]

In cases involving medical science "with respect to which a layman can have no knowledge at all," declared the future Chief Justice of the United States, "the court and jury must be dependant on expert evidence.   There can be no other guide, and where want of skill or attention is not thus shown by expert evidence applied to the fact, there is no evidence of it proper to be submitted to the jury." [13]

We have previously pointed out that the causal relation between the physician's act or omission and the injury complained of must be definitely established; this fact cannot be left to mere surmise. Cases not infrequently arise where there may be an honest doubt as to whether the doctor's act or the disease itself or something else was responsible for the bad result.   An honest expert will ofttimes be found to admit that he cannot say whether the doctor's act or some other cause was responsible.   In such cases the plaintiff cannot recover.   "Where," declared the New York Court of Appeals, "there are several possible causes of injury, for one or more of which the defendant is not responsible, the plaintiff cannot recover without proving that the injury was sustained wholly or in part for a cause for which defendant was responsible. If the matter is left in doubt and it is just as probable that the injury was the result of one cause as the other there can be no recovery." [14]

In order to sustain the plaintiff's burden of proof, "it is not enough," declared Judge Taft in the case previously quoted, "to show the injury, together with the expert opinion that it *might* have occurred from negligence and many other causes. Such evidence has no tendency to show that negligence *did* cause the injury. When a plaintiff produces evidence that is consistent with an hypothesis that the defendant is not negligent and also with one that he is, his proof tends to establish neither." [15]

We shall reserve for later chapters a fuller discussion of expert testimony. The essential elements of a malpractice action have now been stated. The principles discussed seem simple and logical enough; properly to apply them, however, is ofttimes a problem of extreme difficulty. As the New York Court of Appeals tersely said: "The law relating to malpractice is simple and well settled, although not always easy of application." [16]

CHAPTER VIII

APPARENT EXCEPTIONS TO THE EXPERT TESTIMONY RULE

WE have seen that malpractice actions usually revolve about the issue of whether the physician used the requisite skill and employed the approved methods in general use. These are necessarily scientific questions requiring expert testimony for their elucidation. Yet cases may and sometimes do arise wherein the defendant is so palpably at fault, that the lay mind can see it without expert guidance. Such cases are infrequent, but they do occur. "If," said the court in an Iowa case, "a surgeon undertaking to remove a tumor from a person's scalp let his knife slip and cuts off his patient's ear or if he undertakes to stitch a wound and by an awkward move thrusts his needle into the patient's eye . . . it does not need scientific knowledge or training to understand that ordinarily speaking such results are unnecessary and are not to be anticipated if reasonable care be exercised by the operator." [1] In the case last cited the defendant doctor in performing an operation for the removal of adenoids, cut the plaintiff's tongue and loosened her teeth. The verdict which she recovered against him was affirmed. "This," said the Appellate Court, "is not the ordinary case where a practitioner is sought to be charged with liability for alleged improper treatment of some bodily ailment or infirmity. He was employed to remove the adenoids from the plaintiff's throat and there is neither claim nor proof that he did not successfully remove them. His negligence, if any, was in failing to take due care to avoid injury to the undiseased parts in the vicinity of which the operation was performed; and while it may be true that had the operation upon the adenoids been unsuccessful or disappointing no inference of negligence or want of skill would arise therefrom; it does not follow that this rule applies with the same force to an injury done by him to sound and undiseased parts of the plaintiff's person which he was not called upon to treat and did not pretend to treat." [2]

I have had to settle cases where the doctor operated on the wrong foot, the wrong eye and even upon the wrong patient. Whatever else laymen may not understand, at least they know that the wrong patient should not be operated on. Upon such questions they do not need to be told by doctors that the "approved methods in general use" have not been followed. Extreme cases, such as these, however, are happily infrequent.

It is in such extreme cases only where beyond question neither due care was employed, nor the right practice followed that expert testimony is dispensed with. "The question," said the highest court of Indiana, "as to whether or not the physician or surgeon has in a given case exercised reasonable care is *usually* a question for experts, a question of science."[3] Wherever there is any fair question as to whether what the doctor did was proper or improper, a scientific issue is presented. Where such an issue is presented, the plaintiff's burden of proof is not met except by the introduction of expert testimony.

Confusion sometimes arises over this subject, although none should arise. If the trial judge appreciates that however simple the issue may seem to the lay mind as to whether a particular course of professional conduct should or should not have been followed, laymen cannot decide this because while they may think they know, they do not know. What sometimes may seem simple to the layman, ofttimes has been the subject of many volumes of scientific learning and research. If a surgeon were to perform an appendectomy with a rusty can opener, it would not need the opinion of an expert to enable a jury to determine negligence. When on the other hand, any real medical or surgical question is in issue, no one could deny that a jury must have expert guidance. Most cases fall on the one side or the other of this simple line of demarcation indicated by the question: "Is there by any fair view a scientific question involved?" But there are other border line cases.

Needle breaking cases.

The most frequently occurring are those which involve the breaking of surgical needles. Perhaps the most important and the most frequently misunderstood is the Benson case, decided by the New York

Court of Appeals.[4]   The plaintiff there was suffering from rectal trouble.   The doctor who later was to become the defendant in a malpractice action, recommended an operation for ulcers, which he later performed.   While sewing up the incision his assistant's needle broke.   An immediate probing failed to reveal the broken end of the needle adhering in the flesh.   The defendant did not tell the plaintiff or his family or friends of the mishap.   During the twenty months following the operation he steadfastly maintained silence about the broken needle and treated the plaintiff for ulcers, although the symptoms were attributable to the presence of this foreign body.   The defendant neither correctly diagnosed the trouble nor advised the plaintiff to consult a specialist.   Later of his own accord, the plaintiff sought the services of a specialist who probed for and found the fragments of the needle, with the result that the trouble soon cleared up.   At the trial the plaintiff sought to prove his case without expert testimony contending "that the loss of a portion of the needle in an operation coupled with a bad result, standing alone is evidence of unskilled surgery."[5]   The defendant's experts testified that "surgical needles occasionally break, even when the operator uses the highest degree of care and skill."   The plaintiff produced no evidence to rebut this.   The judge charged the jury that the "mere breaking of the needle alone was not necessarily negligence, *but might be some evidence of negligence.*"   There was a verdict for the plaintiff.

Because it considered this charge "prejudicial" the

Court of Appeals reversed the judgment. "The evidence of the first operation," declared Judge Pound, "coupled with the presence of the broken needle in the abdomen standing by itself *might* have suggested that proper care had not been taken and *might* have been enough to put the defendant to his proof. . . . Common sense suggests that the condition discovered by Dr. Saphir (the specialist who removed the needle) was incompatible with successful surgery and medical treatment. But when the evidence of the defendant's surgeons came into the case with a reasonable explanation showing what may happen when the proper degree of care and skill is ordinarily exercised, the possible inference of negligence from the breaking of the needle alone was driven out and the jury should have been so instructed. The rule *res ipsa loquitur* put upon the defendant the burden of going on with the case . . . but in the absence of medical evidence to the contrary, it must be assumed on this appeal that the breaking of the needle was not due to negligence." [6]

I have many times heard astute counsel representing plaintiffs in malpractice actions endeavor to persuade the trial court that the Benson case is authority for their contention that the doctrine of *res ipsa loquitur* is applicable to all malpractice cases, and that expert testimony is not needed, but I have never seen a trial judge misled by this argument. The most that could be said is that the *res ipsa* rule is applicable to cases like the Benson case, i.e., those involving the breaking of a needle, and that even in such cases the fact of the breaking merely puts the defendant to his proof to explain by expert testimony that he followed the approved practice.   Where this is done and such evidence is not rebutted by the plaintiff, a plaintiff's case has not been legally established.

"Ordinarily," said Judge Pound in the Benson case, "jurors would find difficulty without the help of medical evidence in determining the right of a patient to recover against his physician for malpractice based on lack of scientific skill, but the results may be of such a character as to warrant the inference of want of care from the testimony of laymen or in the light of the knowledge and experience of the jurors themselves." [7]   The rule enunciated in this case in no event should be applied to cases other than those involving needle breaking.   I think it should be somewhat strictly construed even in its application to such cases, for we read in the opinion: "Defendant's fault seems to have been the unworthy and unsuccessful attempt to cover up the accident rather than the accident itself. . . ."   My interpretation of this authority has been adopted by all the trial judges before whom I have heard the Benson case referred to.

Several years ago I tried a case in which the defendant doctor removed the plaintiff's tonsils under a local anaesthetic.   He did this by means of a hypodermic injection, but in so doing the needle broke. Immediately upon discovering this, he did all within his power to locate and extract the needle.   He did not immediately tell his patient, fearing that this information would greatly add to her already nervous condition, and hoped that he would find the broken end in the tonsils once they were removed. He did not find it. He thereafter sent his patient home and waited for three or four hours. After she had had some rest and sleep he went to her house and told her what had happened. He immediately arranged to have her taken to a hospital for X-ray and secured at his own expense the services of a well-known physician to remove the broken needle, but although the X-ray recorded its position, the specialist was equally unsuccessful in extracting it. Later the patient sued the doctor who had broken the needle. Her main reliance at the trial was on the fact that the needle had broken. Her sole expert however, was forced on cross-examination to admit that such an occurrence was "possible to happen to anybody. Q. And you don't criticize him for that? A. Not for breaking the needle." There was nevertheless a verdict for the plaintiff. The Appellate Division, however, not only reversed the judgment, but dismissed the complaint. "Malpractice," wrote Judge Martin for an unanimous court, "was not shown by the fact that the needle broke or that part of it remained in plaintiff's body." [8]

In another case which I recently tried in the western part of the state, the infant plaintiff who was attending a public school, was inoculated by the defendant doctor. During the injection the needle broke and part of it remained in the plaintiff's arm. The defendant thereupon asked the plaintiff to step aside until he had treated a number of other children in the line.   Subsequently he had an X-ray picture taken of the arm which revealed the presence of the needle. He tried to remove it, but failed.   He then called in a specialist who operated, but who was likewise unsuccessful in recovering it.   The plaintiff at the trial abandoned her original contention that the mere breaking of the needle was negligence, but rested upon the assertion that the defendant knowing that the needle was broken did not take immediate steps to remove it, but went on inoculating the other children. Her sole expert admitted that he had had needles break in his own practice, but stated that he always removed them "if possible."   On cross-examination he admitted that even in the best hands and under the most favorable circumstances needles will break no matter how much care or skill has been employed. As there was no expert testimony that the breaking was due to any fault of the defendant, or that the delay in operating was improper practice, or that the delay made the subsequent operation necessary, the court on my motion dismissed the complaint.   The Appellate Division affirmed the trial court's judgment.[9]

Other foreign body cases.

Of all foreign body cases those most frequently arising are where a sponge or pack-off has been allowed to remain in the plaintiff's body after an abdominal operation.   These cases involve dramatic possibilities inasmuch as it requires but slight forensic gifts to arouse a jury's ire where it is permitted to examine the bloody exhibit and hear the plaintiff's story (usually punctuated with tears) of the pain and agony suffered while the offending foreign substance was annoying the vitals. I have often looked with extreme discomfort into twelve pairs of eyes glaring threateningly at me while occurrences of this kind were narrated from the witness stand, with no histrionic embellishments omitted. Here if ever, a trial judge must apply the settled rules of law if justice is not to be swept aside by torrents of emotion. For everyone knows that a surgical sponge or other similar foreign body cannot, if permitted to remain, be of benefit to the human system.

To meet cases of this kind the courts have enunciated sound and understanding rules of law. They recognize that a surgical operation is a procedure of the highest difficulty requiring not only a perfect understanding of anatomy, but an agile brain, and quick and steady fingers. They know that the surgeon is working against time frequently in contest with death itself. They know that no two surgical operations are alike, that in each abdomen new problems will be found, that the location of the organs themselves varies in every case. A surgeon has many things with which to concern himself while the operation is in progress. There is the problem of hemorrhage, there is the patient's response to the anaesthesia, there are unforeseen elements to be encountered and to be dealt with. A surgeon is like a general on the field of battle. However thoroughly worked out the plan of action, however perfect the reconnaissance, however complete the maps, however adequate the staff work, however comprehensive the results of his intelligence department, however capable and brave his officers and his troops, something is sure to go wrong, instant decisions will have to be made to meet the immediate emergency and much will necessarily be left to the subordinates.

The courts know that most surgical operations are conducted in hospitals, where the nurses are the employees of the institution, not of the surgeon, and that of necessity much must be left to them, relying on their training and their ability.   There is then always the human equation, and where that is present, error may occur.   The surgeon is busy with his patient, he must rely upon the nurses for many things, for the preparation of the operating room, the sterilization of instruments, the keeping track of what is put in and what is taken out of the open abdomen.   A surgeon after all is only human, he cannot do everything, he must rely on some one.   Realizing these things the courts have formulated fair rules to meet them. Thus when a surgeon follows the usual and ordinary practice of calling for a sponge count from the nurse and relies upon it, he will not be liable if the nurse errs, provided the nurse was the hospital's employee and not his, if the foreign body is so concealed that a reasonable search would not reveal it, and he has made such reasonable search.   If the wrong count is made by his own nurse,—not merely those under his temporary direction in a hospital, but in his immediate employ—of course he is liable for their neg-

ligence on ordinary principles of agency.   But if the
nurses of the hospital miscount, he is not liable for
their mistake.

In the central part of the state a little while ago, I
tried a case involving this interesting principle.   The
plaintiff there had originally suffered from a ruptured
Fallopian tube as the result of an ectopic gestation.
When the defendant doctor operated his first incision
discovered not only the ruptured tube, but an extensive hemorrhage.   Quarts of blood shot into the
peritoneal cavity.   The intestines became distended,
and pushed up towards the wound.   To keep the intestines back the defendant used a number of moist-
ened large packoffs; to the end of each of these there
was attached a tape on which there was sewed a steel
buckle.   As each packoff went in this buckle was
snapped to an artery clamp on the outside to prevent
the pack from being lost in the abdominal cavity.   As
the blood came from the upper abdomen into the
operative field, these packoffs required frequent
changing, and when they were removed they were
taken out and thrown into a pan or on the floor.   The
surgeon was working against time.   He was trying
to and did save his patient's life.

This operation was performed in a hospital, two
of the nurses of which assisted at the operation.
They were not the defendant's employees.   Before
closing the wound the defendant put his hand into the
abdomen to make sure that no packoff was remaining.
His assistant did the same.   After this and before
finally closing the incision the defendant turned and

asked the nurse in charge of the operating room for a sponge count. Thereupon the operating room supervisor told him that the count and tally were correct and that everything was out. He then closed the wound. Now it seems that in getting ready for this operation the nurse had not only prepared large packoffs, but also some of smaller size, such as are ordinarily employed in appendectomies. One of these apparently (although this was never established, except by inference) had been inadvertently rolled up in one of the large packoffs so that when one of the latter was inserted, the small one went in with it, unbeknownst to anyone and therefore was not included in the count and tally. Three months later the plaintiff suffered pain, was X-rayed and the presence of a steel buckle was plainly shown. The defendant surgeon operated and found the abdominal packoff with the buckle attached, both of which he removed. There was an uneventful recovery.

Later the plaintiff sued the operating surgeon claiming negligence in having failed to discover the foreign body at the first operation and in having failed to remove it. Her lawyer thought that the facts spoke for themselves,—*res ipsa loquitur*—and therefore offered no expert testimony. A surgeon of twenty years' experience testified for the defendant that the latter's procedure in all respects accorded with the approved methods in general use; that it was proper practice to rely upon the nurses for a sponge count, and that he knew of nothing that the defendant

could have done which he had not done.   I contended
(unsuccessfully on the trial, but correctly as the Appellate Division and Court of Appeals later decided)
that there was no case for the jury,—no evidence of
negligence, and that the mere presence of the foreign
body did not prove that negligence had been committed, inasmuch as there was no expert testimony
that in leaving it the defendant had departed from
any proper practice, and there was expert testimony
that all that he had done was proper.   The court
nevertheless submitted the case to the jury which
found a $5,000 verdict for the plaintiff.

On appeal to the Appellate Division and the Court
of Appeals, I secured a reversal of this judgment on
the grounds which I had unsuccessfully urged upon
the trial court.   "Plaintiff's theory," said the Appellate Division, "was that the leaving of the packoff in
the abdomen made the lack of skill and want of care
so obvious that expert testimony was unnecessary.
But defendant called an expert who said that proper
and approved methods were used in the operation,
and then inferentially that there was no negligence.
He stated that it would have been unwise for defendant to have made a more extensive search for foreign
substances in the abdominal cavity at the close of the
operation and might have caused paralysis of the
intestines; also that it was proper and customary for
the operating surgeon to rely on the nurse's count of
sponges, packoffs and gauze placed in and removed
from the incision.   Plaintiff did not rebut defendant's
medical evidence that proper and approved methods

were used. The presence of the packoff in the abdomen after the first operation suggested that proper care had not been used, and required defendant to offer proof in explanation. But when defendant's expert witness stated that proper and approved methods were used in the operation, the possible inference of negligence because the packoff had been left in the abdomen was destroyed." [10] This decision was affirmed by the Court of Appeals.

The rule enunciated in this case was sound and is in accordance with the prevailing opinion of this country. Thus, on a similar state of facts the Supreme Court of Massachusetts directed a verdict for the defendant. "As there was no evidence," the court there said, "that the nurses or other persons present and assisting were servants or employees of the defendant, he cannot be held responsible for their failure to keep an accurate count of the sponges inserted and removed, and cannot be held responsible if he did not while performing the operation also keep count of the sponges used. . . . No inference of negligence of the defendant could be drawn from the fact that the sponge was not removed by him before the operation was completed, in the absence of evidence that he then in the exercise of reasonable skill could have discovered it. . . . The doctrine of *res ipsa loquitur* is not applicable to the facts in this case as disclosed by the record." [11]

A verdict for $9,000 recovered on a similar state of facts was reversed by the Appellate Court of Indiana. "It has been expressly held," the Appellate

Court declared, "that a surgeon who performs an operation at a hospital not owned by himself, and who is assisted in such operation by nurses not his employees, but employees of such hospital, is not responsible for the mistake or negligence of such nurses in failing to correctly count the sponges used in such operation, whereby a sponge is left and sewed up in the body cavity of the patient. . . . Proof of a bad result or of a mishap is of itself no evidence of negligence or lack of skill. . . . Medical and surgical science must advance gradually; the correct application of its principles is very largely empirical; it has its errors and its failings as have all things into which the 'human equation enters,' and it would not do to hold as a rule of law, that every physician who administers a dose of medicine, and every surgeon who performs an operation, does so at his peril if the result happens to be not good; that a jury of laymen might mulct him in damages if they as laymen should think that he had been negligent in the matter complained of, although his conduct has been in harmony with well recognized standard methods used by physicians generally in such cases." [12]

Retained drainage tubes.

Cases not infrequently arise in which drainage tubes have been permitted to remain in a patient's body, thereby permitting the wound to close over them. Negligence cannot be attributed to the operating surgeon who inserted the tube where he properly left the aftercare to another (see Chap. IX).

X-ray and other burn cases.

A burn whether caused by X-ray or some other modality, such as the so-called baking machine, makes an ugly looking wound,—one from which a jury may turn with an ominous shudder. The results, catalogued as first, second and third degree burns vary in intensity and probable end result, the latter category ofttimes causing not only a severe sloughing of the tissues, but an injury to the bones or the bone covering. Because of their appearance and their frequent dire results, burns of this character are difficult to defend. The plaintiff's lawyer finds in them tempting material for forensic effort with no infrequent consequences of an ominous character to the doctor sued. In these cases a clear understanding of the legal principles both by the judge and counsel for the accused is essential if even approximate justice is to be achieved. I have found that burns resulting from appliances other than X-ray are by far the most difficult to explain.

A man has a sprain or fracture, "baking" is prescribed, he goes to a physician specializing in this work, he puts his arm or his leg in the oven. He is told by the physician or nurse to let them know if the part being treated feels hot. My experience has been that the patient, feeling that the excessive heat will be beneficial to him, contrary to the instructions given to him, does not advise the doctor or the nurse until after the burn has occurred. Much is made by the plaintiff in actions of this character that the doctor was treating other patients at the same time. As I understand it, in treatments of this kind it is customary for the physician to have one or more booths in his office and to go from patient to patient supervising the treatment.   This custom, however, makes very little appeal to the average jury.

Contributory negligence by the patient will also be found in many diathermy burn cases.   Sometimes the patient will move contrary to the physician's instructions, resulting in spark gap burns, or else (as in the baking cases) he fails to advise the physician whether the treatment is too hot.   Despite the elements of contributory negligence, however, these cases are very difficult to defend.   While in many cases of this character expert testimony is not necessary, yet the charge may be of such character as to make expert testimony relevant; for example, it is competent in these cases to show by expert testimony that it is customary for physicians to treat several patients at one time or even, where the treatment has been laid out by the physician, to delegate the actual treatment to a competent nurse.

In X-ray burn cases, however, the rules are different.   Here the doctor is dealing with a powerful agent, the absolute control of which has not been fully perfected.   In spite of the fact that X-ray has been used for a period of about twenty-five years, there is still a difference of opinion among competent doctors as to the manner in which accurate dosage should be determined.   With the assistance of competent physicists and the improvement in the mechanical devices used in X-ray, the risk to the patient has been materially reduced.   The results of X-ray therapy may be bad, but if the doctor has his machine in order, and has used the proper factors of dosage, the right spark gap distance, the proper amperage, the right filter, the correct intervals between treatments, etc., etc., he is not liable even if a bad result ensues.   In no part of medico-legal jurisprudence have the courts used more comprehension than in dealing with actions of this kind.

One of the best known decisions on the subject was made by the Second Department of the New York Appellate Division.[13]   In that case the plaintiff was suffering from pruritus vulvae et ani, for which X-ray treatment is recognized and accepted.   The defendant doctor gave the first treatment on May 17, 1919, he gave another on May 24th.   The correctness of the factors of dosage and the manner of treatment as testified to by the defendant were not disputed.   But all the experts, including the defendant admitted that if on May 24th (the date of the second treatment) redness of the external parts had appeared and hair had fallen out, that there was an indication that further treatment should not then be given.   The case therefore turned upon a lay question: Was there redness and loss of hair on May 24th or not?   The plaintiff testified there was; the defendant swore with even greater positiveness that there was not.   Had there been nothing else in the case, the Appellate Court declared that there was an issue for the jury to decide.   But this was not all.   It appeared in the

evidence that there "are a few people, probably not
more than one out of every 200 or 300, who are
supersensitive to X-ray treatment, and apparently
that disposition of the patient cannot be known in advance of the test of actual treatment and its results."
"Such cases," said the Appellate Division, "are so
rare that evidently physicians and patients have to
take that risk—the one in administering and the other
in receiving the treatment."   Despite this the trial
judge charged the jury that the result might be considered by them "as some evidence of negligence,"
and was sufficient to cast upon the defendant the duty
or burden of explanation.

Deciding that this was not the law, the Appellate
Division in reversing said: "It having been proven
that specific results might come from proper treatment without negligence on the part of the physician,
that is in the case of a hypersensitive person, the mere
fact that the result did follow the treatment in this
case was in itself no evidence of negligence.   The
case thus presented was merely one where, according
to the proof, the stated result might have followed
from one cause, viz., the defendant's negligence, or
from another cause, viz., plaintiff's hypersensitive-
ness; and therefore, the naked facts of that result
was in itself no evidence of the existence of the one
cause in preference to that of the other." [14]

The case just considered involved X-ray therapy.
The rules governing this are equally applicable to
radiography.   In each class of case X-rays are shot
through the human body, the former for treatment,

the latter for purposes of diagnosis.   The principles underlying the physician's duty are identical.   Thus, in a Pennsylvania case it appeared that the plaintiff was burned as a result of the taking of a number of X-ray pictures.   In effect the trial court charged the jury that they could infer negligence from the fact that the plaintiff had been burned.   The Appellate tribunal reversed the lower court declaring that the charge left "out of account the idiosyncrasy of certain persons to X-ray.   That there is such idiosyncrasy and that it cannot be known until after the X-ray has been used, was shown at the trial." [15]

But there were other errors committed by the trial judge, among which was the manner in which he emphasized the danger of X-ray.   "The court unduly stressed the fact," the Appellate Judge said, "that X-ray is a dangerous instrumentality.   So is a surgeon's knife.   If human ills are to be cured such instrumentalities must be used.   To put upon the medical profession, which must use them, such a burden as financial responsibility for damages if injury or death results, without proof of specific negligence would drive from the medical profession many of the very men who should remain in it, because unwilling to assume the financial risks." [16]

The trial court had permitted the case to be tried upon the theory of *res ipsa loquitur,*—that is, that the thing (in that case the burn) spoke for itself, in other words, established negligence without the need of further proof.   This is the theory as will be recalled, that was so eloquently rejected by Judge Taft

in the case of an operation on the eye.[17]   It is the
theory that in one form or another is advanced so
frequently (and so unsuccessfully) by plaintiffs in
malpractice cases.   Holding that the *res ipsa loquitur*
doctrine has no application to X-ray burn cases, the
Pennsylvania Appellate Judges quoted from the Supreme Court of Arkansas: "The doctrine of *res ipsa
loquitur* does not apply in such cases, because the testimony shows that on account of the idiosyncrasies
. . . one person of a certain type and temperament
would be susceptible to a burn while another person
of a different type under the same circumstances
would not be burned.   Moreover it is shown that
burns do occasionally occur in the ordinary course of
exposure in spite of the highest diligence and skill to
prevent them." [18]

These principles have the approval not only of the
weight of authority in this country but of the United
States Supreme Court as well.   A resident of the
District of Columbia received an X-ray burn.   She
sued the doctor claiming that the burn was in and of
itself evidence of negligence, and that no further
proof was needed.   But this doctrine was rejected
both by the trial court and on appeal.   "Generally
speaking," said the Court of Appeals, "no inference
of negligence can be drawn from the result of the
treatment of a physician or surgeon.   In the absence
of special contract they are not insurers and there
must be evidence of negligence by witnesses qualified
to testify." [19]

At the trial of that case the defendant doctor called

several experts who testified that the type of apparatus used was proper and that the duration of exposure and the manner in which the apparatus was
used was in accordance with the practice of careful
and prudent X-ray operators.   The plaintiff offered
no evidence to the contrary.   "Here," said the Appellate Court, "there was no testimony that the instrument used by the defendant was out of repair,
that the exposures were of too frequent periods or of
too great duration.   Neither is there any evidence of
lack of skill."   Whereas the defendant "introduced
six physicians skilled in that particular branch of
practice whose testimony without exception negatived
the charge of negligence." [20]

X-ray therapy differs, however, from radiography
in this, that in therapy there will needs be an occasional burning of the intermediate tissues in order
that the ray may penetrate to the deep seated point
of the disease.   Such burning may be as inevitable as
the injury to the patient's side occasioned by the knife
which opens the way for the removal of the appendix.
The intermediate results in both cases may be distressing, but they cannot be helped.   This is plain
common sense.   In such cases, although the estab-
lishment of the burn may put the defendant to his
proof, he meets his burden by expert testimony that
the intermediate burning could not have been avoided
if there was to be treatment of the disease.   I remember trying a case involving a deep carcinoma of
the inner side surface of the thigh, in which the
roentgenologist used a cross fire resulting in a fright-

ful burn.   The jury were made to see that the burn
while distressing was inevitable and accordingly found
a verdict for the defendant.

Some conclusions.

Conclusions are tempting things to draw.   The
readiness with which they are drawn, however, is ofttimes unhappily proportioned to the ignorance of the
person who indulges in this exercise.   It was the
speculative tendencies of Galen and his followers and
imitators throughout the middle ages that were responsible for the long night that intervened between
Hippocrates and the protagonists of modern scientific
medicine who based their work upon the Hippocratic
dictum: "To know is science, but merely to believe
one knows is ignorance."

Conscious of my limitations, I nevertheless believe
that we have before us sufficient data on which to
found some accurate deductions on this the most important branch of medico-legal jurisprudence.   I
shall, therefore, endeavor categorically to state the
rules as to the necessity for expert testimony in malpractice actions:

First, in the overwhelming majority of malpractice
cases a plaintiff cannot make out his case without expert testimony.   The necessity for it is the rule, the
dispensing with it the exception.

Second, a bad result does not import negligence,—
the rule of *res ipsa loquitur* does not apply—and
thereby obviate the necessity for expert testimony,

except in the instances enumerated in rules four and five.

Third, in every case in which the point at issue involves a question requiring for its correct solution scientific or expert knowledge, expert testimony must be adduced before a jury can be permitted to consider it. Any question involving in any way the propriety of the treatment, however obvious the question may appear to the layman, requires expert testimony for its solution.

Fourth, there are border-line cases, but the mere leaving of a foreign body does not import negligence, so as to dispense with expert testimony. Usually in such case a plaintiff makes out a prima facie case by merely establishing the presence of the foreign body. This, however, may be fully met by the defendant through establishing by expert testimony that the retention of the foreign body did not result from the defendant's departure from approved methods. Thus, in surgical sponge cases where the surgeon was justified in relying on the nurses' count and had executed a reasonable search himself; in broken needle cases where the proper treatment was used, but it is shown that with the best of care and skill needles break; in X-ray cases where the plaintiff is not shown to be a non-idiosyncratic or where the rays were necessary to combat the disease, and could do so only through the destruction of intermediate tissues,—in these and similar cases if such expert testimony is adduced by the defendant and is not broken down or rebutted by the plaintiff, there is no case for a jury to consider.

Fifth, where a physician's failure to use due care is so obvious that by no stretch of the imagination could a scientific question of any kind be said to be involved, such for example, as where a surgeon undertaking to remove a tumor from his patient's scalp lets his knife slip and cuts off his patient's ear,—expert testimony is not needed.

CHAPTER IX

THE PHYSICIAN'S RESPONSIBILITY FOR THE ACTS OF NURSES, INTERNES AND OF OTHER DOCTORS

THE question suggested by this chapter heading is of great importance to the medical profession. It is especially important to the physician practicing in the large Metropolitan centres where so much of the work is done in hospitals, and in which of necessity much reliance must be placed upon the nurses and medical staff of the institution. But there are ramifications of this topic of equal importance to the rural doctor. A subdivision of the subject will help to clarify it.

The responsibility of an attending physician or surgeon for the negligence of internes or nurses either assisting in the operation or in the aftercare or treatment.

As civilization becomes more complex there is naturally a tendency towards division of labor. In business, in trade and in the profession some men are found adapted to one particular branch of work, others to another. Thus, in medicine there are internists, diagnosticians, dietitians, cardiologists, pediatricians, roentgenologists, otorhino laryngologists, genito-urinary surgeons, traumatic surgeons, general surgeons, specialists of one kind or another in other parts or functions of the body, as well as general practitioners. Now, the most competent man is usually the one most in demand. Some surgeons go from one operation to another as long as their strength holds out. In any department of endeavor it is an economic waste for one who can do what few others can accomplish, to spend his time in doing what hundreds of others can do as well as he, and thereby preclude himself from doing what the many are incapable of accomplishing. The courts have applied these principles to the surgeon and have held that he is not responsible for the after-care performed by internes or nurses not in his employ, unless he has expressly agreed to undertake that work.

The leading decision on this topic was rendered by the courts of Maryland. It there appeared that the defendant Myers had operated on the plaintiff for the removal of the lower third of the right kidney and the bowel. Upon the conclusion of the operation a cigarette drain was inserted within the kidney pelvis. It was the usual drain made of gauze rolled in the shape of a cigarette and so covered with sterilized silk as to assist the blood or other foreign substances to drain from the cavity where it was placed to the outside. The end of the drain and of the two gauze strips protruded several inches from the wound. A stitch was taken in each corner of the incision, the intervening space was left open. After the operation the after-care of the patient was en-

trusted to the hospital internes who were not employees of the surgeon.   The location and character
of the drain were such as to be plainly visible to those
who did the dressings.

Before the patient's discharge from this hospital,
the drain should have been removed, but it was not,
and thus it was five weeks later that the family physician, when the patient returned home, found in this
wound a piece of gauze and some rubberized silk.
Because of the retention of this foreign body the
wound failed to close.   The patient sued the operating surgeon, but the courts sustained the latter in his
contention that he had neither knowledge of nor was
privy to the negligence of the nurses or internes who
did the dressings, and that in a hospital of repute
when a wound is left open the operating surgeon is
not liable for the negligence of those entrusted with
the aftercare.   "At this day," said the Court of Appeals of Maryland, "where it is well known that there
are physicians and surgeons of special skill in particular branches of their profession, it could not safely be
announced as a general rule of law, applicable to such
cases as this, that a surgeon who performs an operation is liable for the negligence of other physicians,
nurses or internes in hospitals in the after treatment,
unless he specially undertakes such employment." [1]

But the court went even further, recognizing the
value of a good surgeon to the community in these
words: "It might be detrimental to the public if such
a surgeon was required to attend to the after treatment, as it would be impossible for him to do so and

perform as many operations as some of them do." [2]
The doctrines enunciated in this case have found judicial acceptance throughout the United States.[3]
The English courts long ago accepted it.[4] The
United States Circuit Court of Appeals has gone so
far as to say that in such cases proof that it is customary for operating surgeons to rely on internes and
nurses in good hospitals is unnecessary, because "reliance thereon by an independent operating surgeon
and by patients therein for the usual care and after
treatment incidental to an operation are matters of
common knowledge and entitled to notice accordingly." [5]

*The responsibility of a physician who acts as an anaes-
     thetist or as an onlooker and who has no control
     over the operation.*

Of course, an anaesthetist is responsible for his
own negligence in selecting an improper anaesthesia
or negligently administering it, or for any other failure to use due care in the performance of the work
assigned him.   But if the operating surgeon is negligent, may the anaesthetist be held equally responsible?   The question was thus succinctly answered by
the Iowa courts: "It is well settled that generally
speaking a physician who merely administers an
anaesthetic to a patient who is operated upon by another is not liable for the negligence of the operating
surgeon." [6]

Thus, in a Kentucky case the plaintiff's excessive
uterine bleeding necessitated the performance of a

laparotomy.   During the operation gauze was placed in the uterus but was not removed.   The defendant was acting as an anaesthetist.   He took no other part in the operation.   "It is a well established rule in surgical operations," said the court in holding the anaesthetist not liable, "that the anaesthetist is directly chargeable with the physical condition of the patient in the operating room and his attention must always be directed solely to administer the proper amount of the anaesthetic and continuing to supply it in just such proportions as will insure the patient's remaining in a comatose condition while the knife is being used." [7]

Even where a physician has advised against an operation, but thereafter consents to act as the anaesthetist during its performance, he is not responsible for the operating surgeon's acts.   This was decided in Vermont where the court said : "Dr. Crane had already advised against any operation at the time and place where it was performed, but his advice had been disregarded and the operation was being performed contrary thereto and was not subject to his control.   Therefore he was not called upon to object to nor to protest against it and hence no inference of approval of it could be drawn against him from his silence in that respect." [8]

It is seldom if ever that an anaesthetist has "control" of the operation.   We have seen how the courts recognize that his attention "must always be directed solely to administer the proper amount of anaes-thetic," [9] and yet he is not a mere dummy at the operation and may have some responsibility therefor if he *observes* something wrong and fails to object.   Thus, in a Federal case the United States Circuit Court of Appeals declared: "Two physicians independently engaged by a patient and serving by mutual consent necessarily have the right in the absence of instructions to the contrary to make such division of service as in their honest judgment circumstances may require. . . .   Each in serving with the other is rightly held answerable for his own conduct, and as well for all the wrongful acts or omissions of the other which he *observes* and lets go on without objection or which in the exercise of reasonable diligence under the circumstances *he should have observed*.   Beyond this his liability does not extend." [10]

The case just cited involved an anaesthetist and a surgeon.   The plaintiff there who was delivered of a child, sued the doctors charging them with causing or permitting vaginal and uterine tears and lacerations, with having failed to remove a part of the placenta, and with such a failure properly to sterilize the instruments as resulted in infection.   Now it appeared that the doctor who later acted as the anaesthetist had had charge of the case before the operation and up to the time when the plaintiff's husband called in the surgeon.   When the latter arrived and made his examination, he concluded that a successful delivery could not be made without instrumentation. It was arranged between the two physicians that the surgeon should handle the instruments and that the doctor who had been in charge before the surgeon

came, should administer the anaesthesia. Whatever the condition of the instruments may have been,
there was no evidence that the anaesthetist knew or
had reason to suspect that they had not been properly
sterilized. His contention therefore, that he was
not liable for any negligence of the surgeon, as the
latter was an independent contractor, was upheld by
the United States Circuit Court of Appeals. Referring to the anaesthetist's alleged responsibility for
the improper sterilization of the instruments, that
court said: "By the exercise of reasonable diligence
under the circumstances should he have known?
Not unless while attentively engaged in his own part
of the service he ought . . . to have entertained a
suspicion that an apparently learned and skillful surgeon was about to commit a gross medical offense,
and to have followed up the suspicion by inquiring
whether his brother had forgotten to sterilize his
hands and his instruments. No unreasonable burden
is imposed by the law." [11]

As to the anaesthetist's alleged responsibility for
the retained placenta, the court said: "When the
after-birth was delivered, Rice (the surgeon) examined it, and found it to be entire and at once had it
disposed of. Morey (the anaesthetist) from across
the bed looked at it and to him it appeared to be intact. Nothing in the record warrants a finding that
Morey knew that Rice had not removed all of the
after-birth. And here too Morey was not bound to
assume in the absence of observable indicia that Rice
was incompetent." [12]

Where, however, a physician merely attends an operation to observe it,—as a spectator—but has no connection or responsibility for it in any way, he cannot be held responsible for the acts of the operating surgeon.[13]

Responsibility of the physician for the substitute whom he sends or recommends.

"A physician or surgeon," one of the most celebrated writers on the law of negligence has said, "is not liable for the negligence of another practitioner whom he recommends or sends in his place when he is unable to attend the patient and whose services are continued under an independent contract, since no relation of agency or employment exists between the physicians." [14]   These views have found acceptance by the courts throughout the United States.   Thus, in Arkansas a Dr. Keller was treating a patient for a dislocated arm.   Before he concluded with the treatment he advised the patient's parents that he was leaving town and that during his absence a Dr. Minor would attend the case.   The parents did not demur. Subsequently they sued Keller for Minor's alleged malpractice.   There was no business relation between these two physicians and the court therefore decided that Keller was not responsible for Minor's treatment.[15]

"If one physician," said the Supreme Court of Montana in a similar case, "upon leaving temporarily the community in which he is engaged in practice recommends to his patient the employment in case of need of some other surgeon who is not in any sense in his employment nor associated with him as a co-partner, he is not liable for injuries resulting from negligence or want of skill in the latter, in case he is employed.   In such case the employment of the latter is under an independent contract and he is solely re-sponsible for the result." [16]   In such a case the Georgia courts declared that "the patient will be pre-sumed to have reposed confidence in the professional capacity of the substitute, not as an agent but as the principal, and will be taken to have relied upon him as a physician to exercise his own knowledge, skill and discretion." [17]

Where two or more doctors treat the same patient, one is not responsible for the negligent treatment of the other, unless he observes or ought to have observed such negligent treatment and by per-mitting it to go on acquiesced in it.

This principle was well illustrated in a Massachu-setts case where the plaintiff went to a hospital to have her tonsils removed by X-ray.   Dr. Jennings was the head of the X-ray department, receiving a salary from the hospital for his services.   The plain-tiff, however, was not treated by Dr. Jennings, but by one Meachen, an X-ray technician.   In performing his work Meachen omitted the use of a filter, as a re-sult of which omission the plaintiff was burned.   She sued Dr. Jennings contending that as he was the head of the X-ray department he was responsible for the technician's negligence.   But the court said:

"Meachen was not employed by the defendant; he was not the defendant's agent or servant. They were fellow employees of the . . . Hospital. The defendant was not responsible for the neglect of Meachen in administering the treatment which was entirely in his control. He did not participate in the operation and was not liable for her injury." [18]

The question most frequently arises where the family doctor calls in a surgeon to operate. The frequency and propriety of such arrangements have been judicially recognized. Thus in a Michigan case, the plaintiff was suffering from certain internal disorders requiring operative intervention. Dr. Bennett, her family physician was authorized to select the surgeon and arrange for him to perform the operation. Dr. Smith was the surgeon selected for this purpose. With the full sanction of the plaintiff it was arranged that Dr. Smith was to operate and that Dr. Bennett and others were to assist. Together with another assistant Dr. Bennett helped to sponge out the blood. That was all he did. During the operation a pack-off was left in the plaintiff's body. She later sued Dr. Bennett claiming that he was responsible for Dr. Smith's neglect. "It is not the uncommon case," said the Supreme Court of Michigan, "of a practicing physician advising a patient to submit to a surgical operation to be performed not by himself, but by some surgeon of reputation, skill and experience, for which operation with the consent of his patient, he makes the necessary arrangements, in performing which he assists the operating surgeon as directed or advised. . . . Neither was employed by the other. Each was required to exercise ordinary skill and care. But discretion and control of the operation were with one man. Whether responsibility for what occurred is rested upon contract or upon negligent performance of duty, there is no rule of law which under the undisputed facts, imputes want of skill or care on the part of Dr. Smith to Dr. Bennett." [19]

But while the physician who calls in a surgeon is not responsible for the latter's negligent acts unless he in some way participates in them, he is under a duty to recommend a competent surgeon. If he recommends an incompetent he does so at his peril. "Where," said the court in an Iowa case, "the physician in charge of a patient calls a surgeon into the case, and assists in the operation by doing what he is directed by the surgeon to do it has been held that he is not liable for negligence in the operation *in the absence of negligence in recommending the surgeon,* or on his own part in assisting him." [20]

But, of course, no physician will be excused who stands by and watches another improperly treat his patient without protest or actually participates in the neglectful treatment. Thus, in a Colorado case the plaintiff who had injured her leg, called in a doctor to determine whether there was a fracture. Not being certain, he called in a second physician. The leg was perceptably shortened and the foot everted, yet both physicians diagnosed the condition as a contusion and advised that an X-ray was unnecessary. Both then continued to treat the leg, but after a time were discharged.   X-rays were then taken and a fracture was revealed.   It was properly decided that both doctors were guilty of malpractice, and that acting in conjunction as they were, each was liable for the other's negligent acts.[21]

"If," said the court in a Montana case, "one observes and lets go on without objection wrongful acts and omissions by the other or if the circumstances are such that he ought to have observed such wrongful acts or omissions he is liable. . . .   If one is guilty of want of ordinary professional care and skill in choosing the mode of treatment adopted, and the other expressly or impliedly gives his approval, there is no reason apparent why the latter should not be held guilty also, for by his acquiescence he fails to give the care and attention which his employment requires."[22]

CHAPTER X

ASSAULT—OPERATIONS WITHOUT CONSENT

A PHYSICIAN or surgeon no matter how experienced, how eminent or how skilled, except under certain conditions which we shall later discuss, can operate or treat only if his patient acquiesces. "Every human being," said Chief Judge Cardozo of the New York Court of Appeals, in the celebrated New York Hospital case, "has a right to determine what shall be done with his own body; and a surgeon who performs an operation without his patient's consent commits an assault for which he is liable in damages. . . . This is true except in cases of emergency where the patient is unconscious and where it is necessary to operate before consent can be obtained." [1] In his usual terse and compact style this great judge, the most profound and philosophical, and with the possible exception of Mr. Justice Holmes, the most celebrated jurist in America, has thus in two sentences summed up the whole law on this subject. And yet there are amplifications and illustrations of this rule which cannot fail to be of interest to the medical profession.

We have seen from Judge Cardozo's words that a physician is justified in operating even without the patient's consent *"in case of emergency* when the patient is unconscious and it is necessary to operate before the patient's consent can be obtained." What the character of such *"emergency"* must be, and what may make it *"necessary"* under such circumstances to operate, Judge Cardozo does not state. But in other jurisdictions the emergency has been defined as one where the patient's life or health is seriously endangered.

Thus, in a Minnesota case the plaintiff gave her consent to an operation on her right ear. During the operation it was found that the condition of the left ear was more serious in that there was a small perforation high up in the drum membrane with granulated edges, and that the bone of the middle ear wall was necrosed. The defendant surgeon called the attention of the family physician to this condition during the operation and they both concluded that the left ear should be operated upon instead of the right. The defendant then performed a very skillful and successful ossiculectomy on the plaintiff's left ear. Later the plaintiff complained of an impaired hearing and sued the operating surgeon. The court held that there was a technical assault, and that while a surgeon during his patient's unconsciousness is justified in operating without the patient's consent to meet an emergency, an emergency was not shown to have existed under this state of facts. An emergency, said the court, means a condition endangering the life or health of the patient, and in that case it was decided that the condition of the left ear drum did not endanger the patient's life or health, and therefore, that there was no emergency present justifying an operation without the patient's consent.[2] This, I think, is a hard case, but it shows how zealously the courts will guard a human being's "right to determine what shall be done with his own body."

In Texas a hard application of the rule is likewise found. There it appeared that a minor child was visiting her elder sister in a city some distance from the child's home. She discovered that the child was having difficulty with its breathing. The physician who was consulted, found diseased tonsils and adenoids, and with the elder sister's consent performed an operation on the child. The consent of the parents was not obtained. While under ether the child died. The parents sued the doctor, and the court held that he was guilty of a technical assault, inasmuch as no emergency existed as to justify the operation without the consent of the parents. "The authorities," said the court, "are unanimous in holding that a surgeon is liable for operating on a patient unless he obtains the consent of that patient, if competent to give such consent, or if not, of some one who under the circumstances would be legally authorized to give the requisite consent. If a person should be injured to the extent that he is unconscious and his injuries of such nature as to require prompt surgical attention, a physician called would be justified in applying such treatment as might be reasonably necessary for the preservation of his life or limb and consent on the part of the injured person would be im-

plied upon the ground of an existing emergency." [3]
The defendant contended with great force that under
the circumstances and in view of the elder sister's authority he was justified in operating, but the court
said: "The law wisely reposes in the parent the care
and custody of the minor child and neither a physician
nor those in temporary custody of the child will be
permitted in a case of this character to determine
those matters touching its welfare." [4]

An illustration of the rule that emergencies justifying operations without consent are those where life or
health is endangered, is found in a New Jersey case.
There the plaintiff had given his consent to the removal of a hernia on the left side. Upon opening
the abdomen the defendant surgeon found a hernia
on the right side far more serious than that upon the
left. He later testified that the condition there was
dangerous both to the life and health of his patient.
When sued for assault, the court exonerated him upon
the ground that the emergency was such as to justify
the operation even without the consent of his patient.[5]

The rule permitting a surgeon to operate without
his patient's consent where the life or limb of the patient is endangered, applies even in the case of minors.
Thus a fifteen year old boy, while crossing a railroad
track in Michigan, was struck by a train and had his
foot crushed. He was taken to a hospital. Upon
his arrival he was sufficiently conscious to give his
name and his address, but he soon lapsed into unconsciousness. The surgeon upon inquiry found
that none of the boy's relatives were present nor re-

sided near enough to be summoned or communicated with. An amputation was imperatively needed then if the boy's life was to be spared. The surgeon therefore proceeded and amputated the injured foot. He was later sued. The court exonerated him. The emergency was such, it was said, that he was justified in doing what he did.[6]

But whether a patient's life or limb is actually endangered may become a hard fought question of fact in any case, a question upon which honest experts may honestly differ. A conscientious surgeon may therefore ofttimes be confronted with a serious dilemma. He may say to himself: "If I do not operate on this newly discovered condition, the patient's life or limb will be endangered! If I do operate I may be sued for assault. What shall I do?" A conscientious man, any man fit to be a surgeon, will under such circumstances do what he thinks is right for the patient and will ignore his own potential danger. All too often, alas, in the medical profession great service is rewarded not with remuneration, but with abuse and an action for malpractice or assault.

A situation differing essentially from those just considered arises where a patient engages a surgeon to relieve him of the condition from which he is suffering, and where there is no definite agreement as to just what the surgeon shall do. In such a case the law implies an authority in the surgeon to take such steps as he may deem necessary to accomplish the desired result, even though in so doing he may be forced to go beyond what either he or the patient may have originally contemplated. Thus in an

Oklahoma case a woman who had suffered from miscarriages, informed her doctor that she wanted to bear children. She stated that she wanted to be "fixed" so that she could do so. During the ensuing operation her doctor found both ovaries sealed and adhesions about the uterus and intestines. He removed the diseased organs and the contiguous infected tissues. The patient later sued him for assault, but the court exonerated him, declaring that the plaintiff's desire to be "fixed so as to have children not only authorized the doctor to diagnose her case for the purpose of discovering . . . the exact cause of her sterility and to make whatever exploratory incisions might be necessary for this purpose. And the mere fact that the plaintiff may have believed that her condition was caused by a laceration of the uterus did not relieve the operating surgeon of the duty of discovering for himself the cause of the physical defect he was called upon to remedy." [7]

The general rule on this branch of the subject was never more clearly stated than by the Ohio courts in these words: "When a patient describes to a surgeon the symptoms of an ailment from which she is suffering and consents to an operation for the relief of her condition she will be presumed to have authorized the surgeon to perform such operation as may be required by the conditions which he finds. And when during the course of the operation it appears to the surgeon to be necessary to extend its scope beyond what was originally contemplated consent to such extension will be implied." [8]

CHAPTER XI

ABANDONMENT

IF a case is properly presented, juries may be made to understand the essentials of a scientific question. If properly elucidated, the most difficult problem of surgery, blood chemistry or pathology, is not beyond their reach. Jurors, after a clear charge of the court will condone a bad result where the doctor has done his best. But there is one thing which they never understand and seldom condone, and that is, the abandonment of a patient by his physician. The issue of abandonment is always a difficult one to handle. Knowing this the plaintiff's lawyer is always glad to have this issue in the case or to make it appear that it is present. It is, therefore, of great importance that the circumstances under which a doctor may, and under which he may not relinquish a case, should be clearly understood by the medical profession.

The simplest rule should be stated first, and that is, that where a physician is dismissed by his patient he is obligated to give up the case, and is, therefore, justified in doing so.[1] But it is the patient and not the doctor who has this power of summary dismissal. Thus, a physician cannot discharge a case and relieve himself from responsibility *without* first giving his patient notice sufficient to enable him to procure other medical attendance.[2]   "When," said Judge Pryor in a celebrated New York case, "a physician engages . . . to attend a patient . . . without limitation of time he cannot cease his visits except first, with the consent of the patient, or secondly, upon giving the patient timely notice, so that he may employ another doctor, or thirdly, where the condition of the patient is such as no longer to require medical treatment, and of that condition the physician must be the judge at his peril." [3]

The courts are zealous as between laymen and their professional advisers to protect the rights of laymen.   Thus, there are many instances in which that which laymen may do, the professional man may not do.   An illustration of this is seen in the right of the patient to discharge his physician with or without cause, but the doctor cannot so easily disassociate himself from his patient.   "Before he can withdraw," the Ohio courts have said, "it is necessary for him to give reasonable notice to the patient in order that another physician may be procured, the character of the services of the physician being such, and his relation to the patient being such that he is not permitted under the law to arbitrarily quit the service at any time without any cause and leave his patient without medical attendance, but he must give reasonable notice though his patient may discharge him at any time." [4]

In a New York case the plaintiff had fractured her arm.   The defendant doctor reduced the fracture and then advised his patient that he was going away for a ten day vacation, at the end of which time he would return. He did not come back until after the expiration of five weeks, when he found that the bones of the plaintiff's arm had slipped from their proper position, and had formed a union with the ends over-lapping. A permanent deformity was present which could not be remedied except by a rebreaking and resetting. There was a verdict for the plaintiff, and the Appellate Division in affirming the judgment said that "when a physician is employed to attend upon a sick person his employment continues *while the sickness lasts,* and the relation of physician and patient continues, unless it is put an end to by the assent of the parties, or is revoked by the express dismissal of the physician." [5]

It would, said the court in a Maine case, "certainly be a dereliction of duty to leave the patient in the midst of critical sickness without care or without suf-ficient notice to enable the party to procure other suit-able medical attendance." [6] No matter what the provocation, a physician who leaves his patient in the midst of the sickness, does so at his peril unless either his patient has dismissed him, or he has terminated the employment upon such notice as to enable his pa-tient to procure another doctor.

Thus in California, a case arose where the plain-tiff was being delivered of a child. It was a difficult delivery and the doctor decided that the use of instru-ments was necessary. Each time when he attempted the insertion of an instrument the patient screamed. After several fruitless efforts he finally told her if she did not stop screaming he would leave.   She did not stop, and he left.   Later another physician was called in.   The first doctor was thereafter sued, and a verdict was recovered against him.   "It is," the California courts declared, "the undoubted law that a physician may elect whether or not he will give his services to a case, but having accepted his employment and entered upon the discharge of his duties he is found . . . to abandon the case only under one of two conditions: First when the contract is terminated by the employer . . . second, where it is terminated by the physician which can only be done after due notice and an ample opportunity to secure the presence of other medical attendance." [7]

These principles like all general rules, however, are not without their exceptions or at least their limitations.   Thus, as we have previously seen (Chap. IX) a surgeon who leaves the aftercare following an operation to a competent hospital staff, is not deemed to have abandoned his patient, unless he has expressly contracted to do this work in addition to the operation.

Again, if after one or more calls the patient tells his physician that he need not come again until he is sent for, the doctor is not liable for an intervening injury where upon the last visit the nature of the trouble could not be diagnosed even after a careful and skillful examination.[8]   When a patient discharges a physician he cannot thereafter hold him liable for an injury occasioned by the doctor's failure to perform some act before the discharge, if it appears that such act should not have been performed before the discharge took place.[9]   So, too, when a specialist is called in as a consultant, it has been held that he is under no duty to continue with the treatment.[10]

CHAPTER XII

SUGGESTIONS ON AVOIDING BEING SUED

ADVICE on keeping out of law suits is like advice on leading a long life,—it may help, but it cannot guarantee the desired result. Many men defy all rules of health and still attain longevity although addicted to tobacco, alcohol, long hours and no exercise. So, too, men who take chances may avoid litigation, yet no one from this would argue that the laws of health should be ignored, or that it is well to neglect whatever may help to avoid being sued.

I shall here endeavor to set forth eleven rules which, if followed, should tend to lessen the likelihood of litigation:

First, the best way to avoid a law suit is not to deserve one. If you give your whole heart and mind and conscience to your cases, and devote your highest efforts in the performance of your duty to your patient, you are likely to avoid trouble. I say you are *likely* to avoid trouble, you cannot be certain to avoid it with some patients no matter what you do. If you have early indications that your patient is of a litigious disposition, you would do well to terminate your relations with him at the first available opportunity.

Second, be careful of your diagnosis. Make sure

before you arrive at a conclusion that you have ascertained, weighed and duly considered every relevant factor, including every detail of the history, and that you have sufficiently considered every special circumstance in the case before you. Be sure not to neglect the help of every diagnostic aid which science has made available. Among the more obvious of these would be the X-ray, urine and blood tests, pathological and microscopical examinations. If you have an honest doubt as to the correctness of your diagnosis, after you have done your best, call in another doctor whom you consider more competent, to confirm your diagnosis.

Third, before consenting to treat or operate upon a patient inquire honestly of yourself whether you are in fact competent to treat or operate for the particular malady which confronts you. If you have an honest doubt upon this subject, call in one of your professional brethren expert in the particular subject involved and see to it that he is employed as a consultant, or that he actually renders the treatment or performs the operation.

Fourth, in all cases of surgery, consider carefully whether in fact a surgical operation is required. In case of doubt, consider whether the less radical rather than the more radical course is the procedure of choice. Never neglect the most rigid attention to all antiseptic precautions. Remember that Lister stressed the necessity of sterile surgery. Give heed not only to the sterility of the operator and his instruments, but to all those who participate in the opera-

tion.   Make sure that a careful sponge count is made.
After calling for the count and before closing the incision, verify the count by a careful manual examination of the operative field.   Put a record of this examination on the hospital chart.   It is wise to have in the operating room a written chart upon which the sponges inserted and removed could be recorded.

Fifth, make sure that all your instruments and appliances are of the most approved design and make, and are in proper working order.   This applies not only to the operative instruments, but to the operating table, chairs and other appliances.   Be careful that your surgical needles are secured from some well recognized manufacturer, and that the needle used is of a size and strength adequate to the demands that will be placed upon it.

Sixth, be careful in your choice of anaesthesias.
Some anaesthesias are proper under some circumstances and not in others.   What one is proper depends upon a variety of circumstances, among which are the strength and age of the patient, the kind of heart he has, etc., etc.   Be careful to inquire whether cocaine has been administered within a short time before the administration of the general anaesthesia.
Wherever possible, inquire also from the patient's history whether he has any idiosyncrasy for any particular form of anaesthesia.   Make sure also that care has been employed in the matter of enemas, and in seeing to it (except in emergencies involving life or death) that the anaesthetic, if it is a general one, is not administered to a patient with food in the stom-

ach.   Consider carefully whether or not a general or a local anaesthetic is the one of choice.   This may depend on a variety of circumstances, including the condition of the patient, the nature of the operation, etc., etc.   It is true, of course, that even where all of these precautions are taken the patient may die while under the anaesthesia.   Death of itself under these circumstances is, of course, no evidence of negligence on the part of the anaesthetist.

Seventh, keep careful records.   This applies not only to the records of the office, but to the records of the operation and of the hospital aftercare.   Before operating, it is wise to have the patient consent in writing to the operation.   This record should contain a brief statement showing that the patient understands the nature of the operation.   Where a patient insists upon leaving the hospital against the doctor's advice, make sure that a statement is signed by the patient setting forth that fact.   When one physician desires, or through circumstances beyond his control is forced to relinquish a case to another physician, cause the patient to consent to this course in writing.

Eighth, one of the most productive sources of litigation is that of X-ray therapy and diathermy.   Do not work in this field unless you understand it.   X-ray therapy and diathermy are highly technical specialties.   New discoveries and new theories are being constantly evolved.   The proper factors of dosage and other factors require a knowledge of the best and most recent thought upon the subject.   Inquire of the patient whether he has been exposed to a previous

X-ray within a time that would render it unsafe for you to subject him to a new exposure.   Consider the fairness or lack of fairness of the patient's skin. Give thought to the patient's occupation.   Do not leave your patient unattended.   Make sure that your machine is in perfect working order and that there are no loose wires with which the patient or his friends may come in contact.

Ninth, keep abreast of the times.   Read the medical journals and the new text books.   Keep your knowledge fresh and up-to-date.   Attend your county medical meetings where you will often hear papers of great scientific value.

Tenth, be conservative in your prognosis.   Unjustifiable promises often lead to disappointment,— sometimes to malpractice actions.   In treating your patient or his family, exercise the highest degree of good faith.   Be scrupulously honest in your advice and treatment.

Eleventh, be tactful and just to your fellow practitioners.   Do not indulge in needless criticism.   The fact that you form or act upon a conclusion different from that of your predecessor affords in and of itself no just basis for condemning his judgment or his action.   Careless remarks, ofttimes unjust, have not infrequently led to litigation.

PART IV

DEFENSES TO ACTIONS FOR MALPRACTICE

CHAPTER XIII

GENERAL CONSIDERATION OF DEFENSES

THE most effective of all defenses is a general denial. The doctor thereby puts in issue every material allegation of the complaint, and he thereby especially denies that he has failed to use the proper and approved methods, and that anything which he has done or omitted is the competent producing cause of the injury complained of.

Where the doctor desires to present new matter through which he helps to relieve himself of liability, he does so by pleading what are called affirmative defenses. Of these the most frequently employed are (a) *res adjudicata;* (b) contributory negligence (in some jurisdictions this defense need not be pleaded); (c) the statute of limitations.

(a) *Res adjudicata.*

This defense is that the matter complained of has previously been considered and decided in the doctor's favor in a previous trial. The New York rules upon this subject are more favorable than those found in any other jurisdiction. It has been held in that state that where a doctor sues and recovers for his professional services, the judgment in his favor in that action is a bar to any later suit by the patient for any alleged malpractice committed in connection with the services for which recovery has been had.   Thus, in the Blair case, the doctor recovered for his services, later the patient instituted a separate action against him for malpractice.   Referring to the doctor's services, the Court of Appeals declared: "But if of value, they could not have been useless; and if of use, they could not have been harmful; and if not harmful, there could not have been *mala praxis* until the performance of them.   Hence, it is *res adjudicata* between these parties that there was not the malpractice, on the allegation of which, in this action, the plaintiff here seeks to recover.   The same question, now raised in this action . . . has once been judicially decided between them, and the judgment remains unreversed. . . .   That question is settled forever between them by that judgment.   It cannot be opened and litigated again, by either of them, in another action." [1]   The fact that the doctor's recovery for services in the first action had been secured by default was deemed by the Court of no importance. But in all jurisdictions, except New York the fact that the doctor's judgment for services was recovered by default "is not a bar to an action by the patient against the physician for damages caused by malpractice in the performance of such services." [2]

Outside New York State the weight of authority is that where a doctor sues for services, the patient may either interpose a defense or counterclaim for malpractice, or otherwise inject that issue into the case, or he may withhold it and bring a separate action against the physician for malpractice, even after the physician has recovered a judgment for professional services.[3]

(b) *Contributory negligence.*

Where the negligence of the patient or that of those who were acting for him caused or contributed to the injury complained of, no recovery can be had. If, however, both the patient and the physician have been negligent and the injuries due to the respective negligence of each are capable of separation, then the doctor is liable for the injuries occasioned by his own want of care or skill. No other negligence on the part of a patient will bar his action against recovery. His negligence must be "contributory negligence," that is, it must have contributed proximately to the injury caused by the malpractice of the physician.[4] In some jurisdictions contributory negligence need not be specially pleaded, but is available under the general issue.[5] In New York it is not necessary to allege contributory negligence in order to establish it as a defense, except where the action is to recover damages for causing death, in which case the defense must be both "pleaded and proven by the defendant." [6]

(c) *The statute of limitations.*

There is so much to be said concerning this defense that we shall devote the following three chapters to its consideration.

CHAPTER XIV

STATUTES OF LIMITATION

DURING the reign of Henry I, when for the first time order began emerging from the "chaos of the Anglo Norman state," [1] the first statute of limitations was enacted.[2]   But it was not until the twenty-first year of the reign of James I that the first general statute of this kind was passed.[3]   In this country all the states now have statutes limiting the time within which actions may be instituted.   Those affecting doctors will here engage our special notice.

The theory underlying all statutes of limitation is that valid claims are usually asserted with promptness and that an undue lapse of time in the assertion of a claim creates a presumption that the right did not originally exist.[4]   Statutes of limitations are "statutes of repose the object of which is to suppress fraudulent and stale claims from springing up at great instances of times and surprising parties or their representatives when all the proper vouchers and evidence are lost or the facts have become obscure from the lapse of time or the defective memory or death, or removal of witnesses.[5]   The underlying purpose of statutes of limitations, said the Appellate Court of Illinois, "is to prevent the unexpected enforcement of stale claims, concerning which persons interested have been thrown off their guard by want of prosecution." [6]

The fundamental characteristic of a statute of limitation "is that it accords and limits a reasonable time within which a suit may be brought upon causes of action which it affects.   Statutes of limitation do not confer any right of action, but are enacted to re- strict the period within which the right, otherwise unlimited, might be asserted." [7]   The legislatures of the several states, varying as they do in their concep- tions of public policy, have prescribed different pe- riods within which an action for malpractice may be begun, and have likewise varied in their laws as to when a physician must sue for his services or be for- ever barred from claiming compensation for them. But all the states have set some time limits for the commencement of such suits.   The term of these statutes, as well as their interpretation and effect may ofttimes become a matter of extreme importance to the doctors, for doctors, like men in other walks of life, may be thrown off their guard by reason of the prosecution against them of stale claims.   Doctors, like other men, lose or destroy their vouchers, books and records, move their offices, get sick or otherwise have their papers in confusion, or find that a lapse of time has obscured their memory of the facts.

CHAPTER XV

WHEN THE STATUTE BEGINS TO RUN

In New York the law provides that an action for malpractice "must be commenced within two years after the cause of action has accrued."[1] A doctor's action for professional services must be commenced within six years after the rendition of the last service.[2] Two years is the legal limitation for the commencement of a malpractice action in many of the states, among which are Massachusetts, Minnesota, New Jersey and Pennsylvania.[3] In California, Connecticut and Ohio there is a one year limitation for the commencement of malpractice actions.[4] And in Maryland the limitation is three years.[5] For states other than those here mentioned, the laws of each state should be separately consulted.

These statutes seem plain enough upon their face, but with them as with other laws difficulty arises in their interpretation. One of the questions most frequently occurring under these statutes is: When does the period of limitation begin to run? This becomes especially important in that class of cases where foreign bodies have been permitted to remain. In such cases does the period start at the time the malpractice was committed or does it begin when it was discovered? Sometimes a negligent act does not result in

injury until some time after it was committed.   In
such cases does the statute begin to run at the time of
the commission of the negligent act or at the time of
the commencement of the consequent injury?

These questions have been asked many times and
have been clearly answered by the courts.   One of
the most important decisions on this subject arose in
New York, where a dentist in extracting a tooth permitted it to drop down the plaintiff's trachea and
lodge in her lung.   It was more than three years after
this that she discovered the fact.   In New York, as
will be recalled, the statute is two years, applicable
alike to doctors and to dentists.   The dentist in the
case under discussion moved to dismiss the complaint
upon the ground that it set forth a cause of action
based on an act of malpractice, i.e., the dropping of
the tooth into the trachea, which act had occurred
more than two years before the commencement of the
action.   The plaintiff contended that the dentist had
known of his negligent act when it occurred and had
concealed it from her in the meantime, and that she
had not begun her suit within the two year period because she did not know the facts until more than two
years had elapsed.   Nevertheless, the court held that
the action was barred.   "There is nothing alleged,"
the court declared, "from which we may infer that
the defendant knew or ought to have known that the
tooth had lodged in the lung. . . .   There is nothing
alleged from which we may infer any intentional
fraudulent misrepresentation of fact as to the presence of the tooth in the lung resulting from letting it

fall down her throat.   At most there was a breach of
professional duty in the operation alleged to have
been negligently performed and in the concealment of
his negligent act.   That was malpractice and the
statute had run against such a cause of action." [6]

In a still more recent New York case, the defendant physician operated upon the plaintiff for appendicitis.   The operation occurred on May 27, 1925.
In a subsequent operation on July 13, 1927, it was
discovered that a pair of forceps had been left in the
plaintiff's peritoneal cavity.   Plaintiff did not begin
her action against the defendant doctor until four
years after the original operation for appendicitis.
The Appellate Division squarely decided that the
plaintiff's action was barred by the two years' statute
of limitations.   The plaintiff there argued that the
statute "should begin to run from the time of the discovery of the malpractice."   The court overruled
this contention saying: "The decisions setting forth
the purpose and effect of such statute are to the contrary." [7]   On appeal the Court of Appeals sustained
the lower court.[8]

In Massachusetts a surgeon was charged with leaving a piece of gauze in the patient's abdomen after
the performance of an abdominal operation.   More
than two years after the operation the plaintiff sued
for malpractice.   The surgeon contended that the
action was barred by the two years' statute of limitations, inasmuch as the action was not begun until
more than two years after the operation was performed, and that the statute began to run from the

date of the alleged malpractice and not from its discovery. The Supreme Court of Massachusetts in sustaining him in this contention, said: "The damage sustained by the wrong is not the cause of action; and the statute is a bar to the original cause of action although the damages may be nominal and to all the consequential damages resulting from it though such damages may be substantial and not foreseen." [9]

Summing up the law of this country a notable authority has declared: "The statute of limitations on an act of malpractice ordinarily runs in favor of the physician or surgeon from the time of the negligent act rather than from the time of the consequential injury." [10]

An exception to the foregoing rules should, however, here be noted, namely, that arising from the suspension of the statute during infancy or other disability. The New York law is that when the cause of action accrues against a person who is insane or imprisoned on a criminal charge, or in execution upon conviction of a criminal offense, for a term less than for life, that the term of such disability is not a part of the time limited for commencing the action, except that the time so limited cannot be extended more than five years by any such disability, or, in any case, more than one year after the disability ceases. An infant may bring an action either within the two year period or, if that has expired before he attains his majority, then within one year thereafter.[11]

CHAPTER XVI

EFFORTS TO EVADE THE STATUTE

THE law abhors a subterfuge. Efforts to accomplish indirectly that which may not directly be accomplished, have always encountered opposition from the courts. This is nowhere more apparent than in attempts to circumvent statutes limiting the time within which actions may be begun.

Ofttimes a plaintiff will decide to start an action for malpractice after the time provided for in the statute of limitations has run. Trouble-makers perhaps gain the ear of the prospective litigant, or possibly the patient decides that the most effective reply to a doctor's suit for the recovery of his professional services is by means of a counterclaim or an independent action, charging the doctor with professional neglect, incompetence or wrongdoing. In such cases the patient is confronted with the fact that the statute of limitations has run against an action for malpractice. Upon inquiry he finds that statutes limiting the time within which actions upon contract may be begun is longer than those limiting the time for the commencement of an action for malpractice. The expedient therefore frequently resorted to in such cases is to sue the doctor for a breach of contract, claiming either that the doctor "agreed to cure" and has not cured, or that he had agreed to perform a certain type of service and had not performed it. But we have previously seen that a physician as a matter of law stands in a contractual relation with his patient. The law defines the contract and prescribes and limits the duties which it entails. It is a failure to comply with these duties which gives rise to an action in malpractice. This is a tort action, not one in contract. To allege, therefore, that the parties entered into a contract,—the very contract which the law implies from the relationship of patient and physician—and that the doctor breached that contract, does not change the true character of the action. It still remains a tort action no matter how the patient or his astute lawyer may choose to characterize it.

Thus, in California a patient claimed that his surgeon had so reduced a fracture of the tibia and fibula as to leave him lame and crippled. The patient brought his action after more than one year had expired since the last treatment by the surgeon. The statute of limitations in California in actions of malpractice is one year. Hence, the plaintiff could not sue for alleged malpractice. How then could he sue at all? His lawyer bethought him that if an action on contract were instituted under the California statute the time limitation had not run. The patient, therefore, after the malpractice limitation had expired, but before the expiration of the contract period, brought his action based on an alleged contract. He claimed that the surgeon (or the hospital which furnished the surgeon) had entered into a contract to furnish proper medical and surgical aid, but had not done so.   But the Supreme Court of California saw through this device and in holding the action barred declared: "Notwithstanding the elaboration with which the plaintiffs have undertaken to set forth the terms and provisions of their . . . contract, we are of the opinion that the gravamen of this action consists in the alleged negligent acts of the chief surgeon . . . consisting in his unskillful setting of the . . . plaintiff's injured limb by reason solely of which the plaintiff's alleged injury and damage arose. . . . The fact that the parties stand in contractual relation to each other does not operate to change the rule or extend the time for the commencement of such actions."[1]

In Illinois the statute of limitations for malpractice is two years.   A plaintiff in that state sued her doctor claiming that he had undertaken to treat her for the cure of the illness from which she was suffering, and that in disregard of his duty he had so negligently and unskillfully treated her as to cripple her for life.   Her action was not begun until more than two years after the last treatment.   She claimed that her action was based on contract and therefore, was not barred by the two year period.   But the Supreme Court of Illinois did not sustain her, and in holding her action barred declared: "An examination of the declaration discloses that the plaintiff is endeavoring to recover for injuries resulting from the alleged negligent and unskillful treatment accorded her without relying on any contract other than the contract which the law implies and which obliges a physician to use reasonable care and skill in the treatment of the plaintiff without reference to any contract of hire. We think . . . that actions for malpractice and cases of this character have always been held to fall within the personal injury class as far back as Blackstone." [2]

Quoting from a well-known authority, the Supreme Court of Tennessee declared: "Where a statute limits the time in which an action for 'injuries to the person' may be brought the statute is applicable to all actions, the real purpose of which is to recover for an injury to the person, whether based upon contract or tort in preference to a general statute limiting the time for bringing actions *ex contractu.*" [3]

The courts are quick to prevent patent efforts to evade the statute. Where the cause of action is sought to be alleged as one in contract which in reality is one in tort, the courts discern that the real purpose of the pleader is to state a case which is not barred by the longer statute and which would be barred by the shorter statute applicable to malpractice actions. An illustration of this is found in New York where contract actions are barred only after six years, but actions for malpractice must be begun within the two year period. The plaintiff in a case arising in that state alleged that a doctor, in consideration of $150 agreed to remove a duodenal ulcer, but neglected to perform his part of the contract by failing to remove the ulcer as agreed. $50,000 damages were asked. If the case was one in malpractice he was barred by the two years' statute of limitations.

If it was in contract the six years' statute had not yet run. The court granted a motion to dismiss the complaint, holding that it was really based upon malpractice although a contract was alleged. "While," said the court, "in the complaint now under consideration, neither lack of skill nor negligence is charged, the basis of the charge is 'improper performance of the work to the personal injury of the plaintiff.'" Further, in support of its conclusion the court stressed the fact that the damages were in an unliquidated sum. "The damages here demanded," the court said, "namely, $50,000 for pain and suffering, are not suited to an action for breach of the alleged contract." [4] In another New York case the court said: "The nature of the charge of malpractice is not changed by failing to sufficiently state it in necessary detail, or by putting in language suitable to the statement of a cause of action in contract, omitting the usual allegation as to absence of skill and negligence." [5]

In some states the legislatures have taken a hand. Thus, the Massachusetts statute reads that "actions of *contract or tort for malpractice* against a physician or surgeon" must be brought within two years after the cause of action arose.[6]

In Minnesota the Finch decision led to a change of the statute in that state. In that case the plaintiff sued his physician for negligence in the setting of a dislocated hip. The complaint charges that the physician "undertook to set and heal" the hip. The defendant doctor demurred to the complaint upon the ground that the cause of action was barred by the statute of limitations in that it had not been commenced within two years after the cause of action arose. But the court held that the action was not barred, for the reason that the complaint set forth a cause of action on contract, which was not barred until six years after the accrual of the cause of action. The cause of action, said the court, "could not be maintained without pleading and proving the contract. The complaint here does plead the contract by alleging the plaintiff employed the defendant to set and care for the joint and that he undertook to do so. The six years' limitations applicable to actions upon contract applies." [7] Seeing the palpable injustice of this decision, the legislature of Minnesota shortly thereafter amended their statute so as to provide that "all actions against physicians and surgeons for malpractice, error or mistake or failure to cure, *whether based on contract or tort*" must be begun within two years.[8]

PART V

EXPERT TESTIMONY

CHAPTER XVII

WHAT EXPERT TESTIMONY IS

PREVIOUSLY in this book we have pointed out that a plaintiff cannot (except in those exceptional cases discussed) recover against a physician for malpractice without the aid of expert testimony. The importance of the subject is, therefore, apparent. It is important to the doctor who is sued, it is important to the prospective expert, it is important to the lawyer who calls him.

Perhaps in no field of medico-legal jurisprudence has there been so much loose thinking, talking and writing as in this one. In no field have there been so many superserviceable and ill-considered proposals for reform. It might, therefore, be well to begin this chapter with a few elementary statements.

The purpose of a trial is to decide the issue between the parties. This is done by ascertaining the facts. Upon the facts the court or jury renders its decision or verdict. The facts in issue are those which are offered on one side and denied on the other.[1]

Facts ordinarily denote acts, events or occurrences. Thus, what the witness has seen, or heard, or done, constitutes the matter about which he may testify, provided that his evidence may not be inadmissible for other reasons. But what the witness thinks about what he has seen, or heard, or done,—his opinion about them—is not admissible. It is the function of the witness to furnish the facts. What is to be thought about them is for those who are to weigh and decide upon them. This function of weighing and deciding upon the evidence belongs to the court or to the jury (if it be a jury trial) guided by the court's instructions. But a fundamental exception to this rule of not permitting a witness to express his opinion is made with respect to questions of science and art. Upon such questions the opinion of persons "specially skilled in any such matter are deemed to be relevant facts." [2] It is in this category that expert medical witnesses are found.

The reason why experts are permitted to give their opinions is that by reason of their special knowledge and study they are qualified to have an opinion about facts in a domain wherein a judge or a lay jury lacks special skill and knowledge. Scientific facts would be meaningless to the lay man without the enlightenment which is shed upon them by one who understands them. How, for example, could a judge or jury unaided, reach any intelligent decision as to the stress and strain upon the cables holding a suspension bridge? Without the benefit of the opinion of an engineer or bridge builder no rational decision could be reached. Similarly how could a judge or jury form any intelligent determination as to the proper size, character or application of a splint, or the proper location or depth of an abdominal incision, or the proper thing to be done or left undone in any field of medicine or surgery, without the opinion of a doctor or a surgeon?

Expert testimony, the Oklahoma courts have well said, is "admitted because the witnesses are supposed to have peculiar knowledge upon the subject of inquiry which jurors generally have not, and are thus supposed to be more capable of drawing conclusions from facts and basing opinions upon them than jurors generally are presumed to be." [3]   Such testimony is allowed when "the jury cannot be supposed to comprehend the significance of facts shown by other testimony, which needs scientific or peculiar explanation by those who do comprehend it." [4]   This rule, like most rules of law, is based upon obvious good sense.

CHAPTER XVIII

WHAT CONSTITUTES AN EXPERT

WE have seen that expert testimony is admitted because those who are allowed to give it "are supposed from their experience and study to have peculiar knowledge upon the subject of inquiry." [1] It will be, therefore, with a feeling of surprise that we shall see how little of "experience" or "study" or "peculiar knowledge" has been demanded by the courts in order to qualify a so-called expert to testify as such. This is one among many reasons that has led to the frequent strictures both upon experts and expert testimony.

While applauding the advances made by scientific medicine in the past fifty years and the improvement in expert testimony, the writers of one learned work declared that "even so there is much improvement to be desired, and expert testimony has still a reputation for uncertainty and difference which better methods of presentation of their really valuable testimony before the tribunal will finally overcome. Among the evils of the present system is that in some departments of legal medicine, physicians who are really not experts in the true sense of the word can still qualify as such. A professorship of therapeutics and insanity in an unimportant medical school, the honorary position of consulting physician to an asylum, or the position of a coroner's physician does not really qualify a physician as an expert alienist or pathologist, and yet the court generally recognizes such nominal insignia of office as evidence of fitness to testify, though the professor of therapeutics may have no medical knowledge of insanity, though the physician may never have visited the asylum to which he has been made consultant by courtesy, and though the coroner's assistant may have been created by purely political influence, with no regard to his attainments as a pathologist." [2]

When a witness is placed upon the stand as an expert, the evidence as to his alleged qualification is furnished through his own testimony.[3] The trial court determines whether or not he is in fact qualified.[4] In examining the decisions of the various courts an amazing liberality in determining expert fitness is discoverable. Thus, in Alabama a physician who had received his doctor's license, had practiced one year, had then been a lawyer and for sixteen years had not practiced medicine, but continued to keep up his medical reading, was allowed to testify as an expert.[5] In Illinois a graduate of a chiropractic school was permitted to testify as an expert in a case involving an injury to spinal vertebrae.[6] But perhaps as striking a case as any, occurred within the writer's own experience. In that case the writer's former partner was defending a doctor for malpractice. The question involved was whether the defendant doctor during the performance of an ethmoidectomy had permitted one of his instruments to penetrate from the nasal to the orbital cavity and had thus severed the optic nerve, thereby causing blindness. The plaintiff called a twenty-six year old physician as one of his experts.[7]   The following excerpts from his cross-examination will prove of interest:

"Q. Have you testified often in suits that have followed operations? A. I have. . . .

Q. The more people hire you, the better you like it? A. Yes, sir.

Q. And the more they pay you, the better it pleases you? A. Absolutely.

Q. Well, don't you call that a professional testifier? A. No, sir, it is all in connection with my general practice.

Q. Well, you are a professional testifier as a side line then, aren't you? A. Yes, sir.

Q. You never operated a major operation on the abdomen, have you? A. Not myself.

Q. But you would assume to undertake, wouldn't you, tomorrow morning, to go into court before a jury and testify as an expert as to how an abdominal operation should be performed? A. If the case were just, I would.

Q. Let us assume the case was just, in your opinion; you would do that? A. Yes, sir.

Q. You have never operated an operation on the brain, have you? A. No, sir.

Q. You would go into court and before a jury and testify on operation of the brain, wouldn't you, if you were hired? A. If the case were just.

Q. And if you were hired? A. If the case were just and I were hired, I would."

But this young man who had only been admitted to practice three years, who was not a member of any hospital staff, who was in no way an eye specialist and who never in his life had performed an ethmoidal operation, was permitted to give an opinion that the defendant's improper practice had caused blindness. On appeal the court held that he was competent to give expert testimony.[8] This decision, however, should not surprise us coming as it does from a jurisdiction where the highest court has stated that "if a man be in reality an expert upon any given subject belonging to the domain of medicine, his opinion may be received by the court, although he has not a license to practice medicine." [9]

It seems universally to be held that "the trial court must be left to determine absolutely and without review" the question of whether or not a particular expert witness possesses the required qualifications.[10]

This tendency towards a minimum requirement of knowledge and experience for expert witnesses has been applauded by some writers of great authority. Thus, for example, Professor Wigmore writes: "The liberal doctrine should be insisted on that the law does not require the best possible kind of witness, but only persons of such qualification as the community daily and reasonably relies upon in seeking medical advice. Specialists are in most communities few and far between; the ordinary medical practitioner should be received on all matters as to which a regular medical training necessarily involves some general knowledge." [11]

The fact that one essaying the rôle of expert witness need not have special knowledge or experience

covering the particular subject about which he is asked
to give opinion evidence seems, as we have said, generally to be held.   Yet such a rule, in my opinion, is
an exceedingly unjust one.   It permits a man to criticize and condemn the work of another physician without having sufficient knowledge or experience to enable him to make a just criticism or condemnation.
It allows a physician of long years of indefatigable
labor and arduous devotion to a specialized field, to
be assailed and injured by an incompetent tyro.   It
is an encouragement to a certain class of lawyers and
to the "professional testifiers" among the medical
profession.   It permits a plaintiff with an unjust case
to supply a necessary link in a chain of proof and thus
to make out a prima facie case where no real honest
prima facie case exists.   The venal and incompetent
expert,—the pseudo expert rather—is the cause and
the justification for a large share of the public criticism which of late years has been leveled at expert
testimony in general.

Various remedies have been suggested,—most of
which, as is so frequently the case with our reformers
—are presented through the medium of new legislation.[12]   Judging by their import, most of these legis-
lative panaceas appear quite evidently to have been
conceived either by laymen, or by lawyers who have
had a very slight experience in the courts.   Thus, it
has been proposed that only official experts be allowed.   But America's experience with "officials" in
general is not such as to excite enthusiasm for this
proposal.   Professor Wigmore condemns such a

plan as "futile, first because it interferes with the traditional right of the parties to adduce such evidence as they think useful; and secondly because it would commit the fate of such issues completely to a body of men who, under certain local political conditions, would be wholly unreliable, and the new state of things would be worse than the old." [13]

A bill embodying something of this plan five years ago was prepared for the American Medical Association. It provided that a party might call either his own experts or might petition the court for the appointment of "such expert witnesses as in the opinion of the trial judge may be proper." To these experts were to be submitted the "facts" upon which their opinion was sought, and this was to be done in advance of the trial. They were to be given the right to examine witnesses under oath and later these official experts were to submit to the court "the problem" concerning which their expert opinion was sought. They might later be cross-examined in court, but their qualifications were not to be "open to attack," and their official status was to be recognized by the direction that the "judge or jury" in weighing the relative value of the testimony of the private and official experts, "shall consider and give due weight to the methods of their respective appointments, whether by the court or directly by any party or parties." [14] The readers of the New York State Journal of Medicine may recall my criticisms of this proposed legislation. [15] Among other glaring defects in the proposal, I pointed out that to allow official experts to examine witnesses, provided "for what amounts to a preliminary trial to be presided over by a doctor, who though excellent in his own profession may have a very hazy knowledge of the rules of evidence, and the methods of eliciting testimony.   He might do well or ill according to his particular ability.   It would be strange if he did not elicit much hearsay or other incompetent proof upon which he would, although he should not, base his opinion.   Such a course would immeasurably increase the complexities of a law suit and would result in that worst of all evils, the law's delay." [16]

I further pointed out that "the provision that the hypothetical question should be submitted to the experts in advance of the trial, has the obvious defect, that while it may represent that which the lawyer presenting it may hope to prove, it may not represent at all that which at the trial he would succeed in proving, and hence the whole hypothesis upon which the expert is invited to express his opinion would be false or faulty." [17]

Another expedient which has ofttimes been suggested is that when a scientific fact is in issue that it be decided by an official jury of experts.   This proposal has well been criticized by Professor Wigmore, who declares it to be "wholly impracticable in our country, first because the jury system constitutionally cannot thus be interfered with, and secondly, because in virtually all litigation the scientific fact is seldom more than a part of the issue, and therefore, cannot be easily segregated for the purpose of being committed to a second and subsidiary jury." [18]

Still another suggestion is that the court on its own

motion wherever a scientific question is in issue, should be allowed to select and call its own experts.   Professor Wigmore thinks that "this expedient would remove most of the present abuses." [19]   I strongly disagree with him in this conclusion.   The fallacy of such a proposal was never better exposed than by the late Judge Willard Bartlett of the New York Court of Appeals, who in a paper read before the New York State Medical Association thirty-one years ago, declared: "I believe that justice in the United States is generally well and honestly administered; but such a thing is conceivable as that a judge might unwittingly appoint incompetent official experts who were anything but representative of the best elements of the medical profession.   In what position, then, might a physician, sued for malpractice find himself, if condemned by their opinions and unable to exonerate himself by calling as witnesses his non-official brethren whose testimony would demonstrate that the appointees of the court were wilfully wrong or ignorantly mistaken?   A man may be a good judge of law and yet be a poor judge of doctors.   I should be very sorry to be treated by the physicians of several able judges whom I have known in past years; and yet I am certain that in each case, his physician would have been the first either of these judges would select for any official medico-legal preferment within his power to bestow." [20]

Perhaps as fair, as intelligent, and as reliable conclusions upon this subject of expert testimony and its evils as have been stated, came from the pens of a special committee of the New York State Bar Association acting in conjunction with the Medical Society of the State of New York and the Homeopathic Medical Society of this state in the year 1909. The remedy for existing evils, this Committee reported "lies with the Bench and the Bar rather than with resort to restrictive legislation. Primarily with the Bench—not the trial Bench alone, but the Appellate Tribunals as well, it is within the power of judges at Nisi Prius, to require a greater degree of competence upon the part of persons claiming to be experts by the single but effectual method of defining to a jury with force and precision the distinction between a witness proven to be thoroughly qualified to speak upon the subject regarding which his testimony is offered, and one whose claim is predicated principally upon the fact that he is paid to do so. If trial judges will pursue this course and are sustained in so doing by the Appellate Bench, courts of justice will be rid of corrupt and worthless so-called experts, provided the judges are animated solely by the wish to see justice properly administered." [21]

Here is a practical proposal. If judges when they have before them a paid incompetent posing as an expert, were, when they charge the juries, to analyze his alleged qualifications as well as his mercenary motives in giving his so-called expert testimony, justice would far more frequently be done. The power and capacity of English judges in this field is not the least of the reasons for the high reputation of English courts.

In the meantime, and until our judges exert more

fully their prerogatives, there is an age-old, but never outworn weapon by which an honest man may be defended against the assaults of an expert whose opinion has been bought and paid for in order to swear through an unjust case. I refer, of course, to cross-examination. This fascinating, difficult and immeasurably important part of the trial lawyer's work has well been referred to as an "art." It is an edged tool, but like all weapons that are sharp it may cause injury to the wielder rather than to the object of the blow. Some lawyers use it like a bludgeon, some handle it as a broad sword, others as though thrusting with a shining rapier. In his work on the "Art of Cross Examination" Francis Wellman has contributed fascinating illustrations of its use as well as its abuse. Yet while this subject may be studied in the books, it never can be learned there. Natural aptitude plus large experience is necessary. To modernize the metaphor employed a few lines back, cross-examination is a weapon more likely to explode in the unskilled hands of the assailant than to destroy the enemy. "When," Mr. Wellman has well written, "the public realizes that a good trial lawyer is the outcome, one might say, of generations of witnesses, when clients fully appreciate the dangers they run in intrusting their litigation to the so-called 'office lawyers' with little or no experience in court, they will insist upon their briefs being intrusted to those who make a specialty of court practice, advised and assisted if you will by their own private attorneys." [22]

CHAPTER XIX

THE HYPOTHETICAL QUESTION

THE method by which the opinion of an expert witness is elicited is through the medium of a hypothetical question. This question assumes the existence of such facts as counsel who asks it may embody in his question, but the facts assumed can be those only which the judge determines have fairly been established by the evidence.[1] "If the hypothetical question is clearly exaggerated and unwarranted by any testimony in the case the objection to it should be sustained." [2]

It is the province of the expert to express an opinion on one or more elements of the case, not upon the merits of the case itself.[3] In a malpractice action, for example, "the question whether a physician has in a given case adopted the proper treatment is one in which the opinion of medical men may be received in evidence and they may state whether in their opinion the treatment was proper or not; whether it was in conformity with the rules of the profession." [4] Thus, in the case just quoted from, the expert was asked whether the application of splints by the defendant was "unskillful and negligent." The allowance of the question was held error, and the court upon appeal said: "The distinction between improper treatment and negligent treatment is not as broad as it is vital. Improper treatment by a surgeon might be due to an error in judgment of a skilled surgeon honestly and carefully exercised and not constitute negligent treatment." [5]

An expert witness may not be asked his opinion as to the existence or non-existence of facts; it is the jury's province not his, to determine that. The question "should be put to the witness hypothetically whether if certain facts testified to as shown to be within his own personal knowledge are true he can form an opinion, and what that opinion is. The jury will then be instructed, if the truth of the facts is contested, first, to consider whether the facts upon which such opinion rests is proved to their satisfaction, and if it is then to give such weight to the opinion resting on it as it deserves. But if the fact is not proved then to give the opinion no weight." [6]

Where certain facts are not in dispute the question should fairly reflect such undisputed facts.[7] But "if some of the facts are in dispute, then each party may frame his hypothetical question to include the facts as he claims the evidence shows them to be." [8]

The foundations of an expert's opinion are the facts upon which he predicates it. If the facts upon which that opinion rests are destroyed, his opinion must fall with them. The object of an hypothetical question is to let the jury know the alleged facts upon which the expert bases his opinion, so that they may in considering the case determine whether the facts upon which the expert relied, are supported by the evidence.   The question, therefore, should not contain facts having no foundation in the evidence, nor should it exclude undisputed facts which are material. "I believe," said Judge Morse in a Michigan case, "all the undisputed facts of a case must be included in a hypothetical question, both as a matter of sound principle and of reason and justice. . . .   To permit . . . a culling of facts to suit the purposes of conviction, to be propounded in hypotheses to experts, and thus to instruct the jury that the only way to contradict the opinion of the experts is by the opinion of other experts, is to deny a fair trial." [9]

There is no more fertile field for the facile legal trickster than in the propounding of a hypothetical question.   It is here that a capable and practical judge may do much to aid the true administration of justice.   "The Court," Professor Wigmore writes, "may well interfere to prevent questions which are under the circumstances practically valueless, and are either intended or fairly likely to mislead the jury." [10]

In an experience covering the handling of hundreds of hypothetical questions, I have found that judges exercise a fair and intelligent discretion.   The procedure which I follow and which usually was approved, was to wait until the expert had been asked if he could express an opinion based upon the facts stated in the question of my adversary, and if the expert said he could I then (if the question seemed faulty) objected.   My objection was usually based upon one of two grounds: either that the question had omitted certain material and undisputed facts (which

I then enumerated) or that the question contained facts which there was no evidence at all to support. The judge then usually forced opposing counsel to include the omitted facts or to exclude those unproven. When the question was thus reformed, it not infrequently happened either that the doctor could not express the opinion which he had been called to express, or that he was far less certain about it than he was when he was predicating it upon the original hypothesis.

It is upon the proven facts that the opinion must be predicated. Hence, it follows that it may not be based upon the opinions of others. It must be found upon facts, not opinions. Where, therefore, a hypothetical question was asked which embodied the opinion of another expert who had very recently examined the plaintiff, it was held improper.[11]

The facts upon which the opinion of the expert is sought must be proven, but they need not be proven by other witnesses if the expert himself has personal knowledge of them, and can, therefore, testify as to those facts of his own personal knowledge. The expert in such a case occupies a dual rôle of fact and expert witness. Where he has personal knowledge of all the facts upon which his opinion is predicated, the hypothetical question may be dispensed with, provided he has previously testified as to those facts. Thus, for example, where the physician is asked: "Did you examine the body?" and he answers "Yes," he may then immediately be asked: "State your opinion of the cause of death," without first asking a hypothetical question embodying all the premises for his conclusion. The reason for this, Professor Wigmore says, is "that on cross examination each and every detail of the appearance he observed will be brought out and then associated with his general conclusion as the grounds for it, and the tribunal will understand that the rejection of those data will destroy the validity of his opinion." [12]   If, for example, it should develop that his opinion is based wholly or in part upon something which he learned out of court from some one else,—hearsay—his opinion will be stricken out.

Where, also, several experts are to be called and all are present during a reading of the hypothetical question to the first witness, the others may be asked if they heard the question read and if they did, may be permitted to express their opinions without the need of repeating the question to each witness.[13]

As we have already said, the use of hypothetical questions has been much abused. They have been condemned by many thoughtful students of the law. Thus, Mr. Wellman writes: "One of the greatest vices of expert medical testimony is the hypothetical question and answer which have come to play so important a part in our trials nowadays. This is perhaps the most abominable form of evidence that was ever allowed to choke the mind of a juror or throttle his intelligence." [14]   Mr. Wellman finds himself in the good company of Professor Wigmore, who says: "The hypothetical question must go as a requirement. Its abuses have been so obstructive and nauseous that

no remedy short of extirpation will suffice. . . .
The hypothetical question, misused by the clumsy and
abused by the clever has in practice led to intolerable
obstruction of truth." [15]

Despite these strictures, the learned Professor ad-
mits that the hypothetical question "is one of the few
truly scientific features of the rules of evidence." [16]
I agree with this latter statement, indeed I fail to see
how a scientific issue could properly be decided without questions of this kind. I agree that the use of
these questions is frequently abused in practice,—so
are scalpels and gavels, but that is not a sufficient
excuse for their total abolition, although it may be an
argument for confining them to those who know how
to use them.

CHAPTER XX

THE USE OF MEDICAL TEXT BOOKS

IN a trial involving a medical issue, much will be seen and heard of medical text books, but many lawyers and some judges seem a little hazy as to how they may be used.

The universal rule is that the "contents of scientific books cannot be read to a jury for the purpose of establishing the facts or establishing the deductions stated in them." [1] The reasons for excluding such books are "because of the unsettled condition of the science; because the language employed is technical, and hence is not within the understanding of men of common experience, because of the difficulty of determining what books are or are not of good authority; because such books are written without the sanction of an oath, and the authors are not liable to cross examination; and lastly because such books are but hearsay evidence of matters about which living witnesses could be called to testify." [2]

This rule has not escaped criticism. Thus, Mr. Taulane has written: "To allow an expert to testify from his reading of standard authorities alone, and yet at the same time to exclude such works as original evidence, seems to be a distinction without a difference. Any one familiar with the so-called expert well knows that the great majority of them specially qualify themselves before trial by reading the standard authorities. In fact, few of them who appear at the trial of causes are competent to form an independent opinion of their own. If they could not refer to the authorities, few of them would attempt to qualify as an expert. Their testimony is a substantial 're-hash' of what they have read. Who for a moment would accept the opinion of the average expert in preference to the statements of such a standard authority as Taylor's Medical Jurisprudence or other similar works?" [3]

Professor Wigmore also believes that text books should be admitted as evidence. The guarantees of accuracy of such books, he says, "at least are greater than those which accompany the testimony of so many expert witnesses on the stand. The abuses of expert testimony, arising from the fact that such witnesses are too often in effect paid to take a partisan view and are practically untrustworthy are too well known to repeat. It must be admitted that those who write with no view to litigation are at least as trustworthy, though unsworn and unexamined, as perhaps the greater portion of those who take the stand for a fee from one of the litigants." [4]

An analysis of these criticisms might well lead to the conclusion that they are founded upon a general disapprobation of expert witnesses rather than the rule which rejects text books as evidence. No one with much actual court experience in the trial of causes, including medical issues, could find himself in accord with Mr. Taulane or Professor Wigmore. The following, among other reasons, might be cited against their theory: (a) What guarantee would there be that the edition of the book read from was the most recent? Authors frequently change their views on further study or as the result of new experiments. It might well be then, that the book read from did not at all express (at the time of trial) the opinion of the man who wrote it. (b) Medical text books frequently treat of specific medical cases with specific histories, and set forth conclusions based upon special facts. What, therefore, appears as the statement of a general principle may not in fact be such, but may in reality apply to special cases which resemble, but which are fundamentally dissimilar to that which is the subject of the litigation. One or two factors or symptoms in the latter might be such as would cause the author (if he were present to be cross-examined) to deny that his statement in his text book had any application to the case on trial. (c) Text books are usually written in a style and technical language which the lay man could understand only if he read them with the aid of a medical dictionary,— and often not then. The jury might be impressed, but not enlightened. (d) Jurors are seldom competent to judge between the relative merits of good and bad medical authority. They might be much impressed by some ancient volume on "midwifery," and think but slightingly of the most recent authority on gynecology or obstetrics.

I believe that the rule which excludes medical text

books as evidence like most rules of law is based upon good sense. I think that trial lawyers of experience in this field will agree with me. But whether they do or not, the weight of authority is to the effect "that books of inductive science, within which are standard medical works are not admissible as affirmative evidence." [5]

Not only is it not permitted to read from medical books to the jury, but no medical expert will be permitted on his direct examination to refer to such books for the purpose of bolstering up or strengthening his testimony. "It is well established," the New York courts have said, "that a party calling an expert cannot read from medical works on inductive science and ask his expert if he agrees with the statement of the author or if it accords with his experience." [6]

Thus, in one case the plaintiff called his attending physician as a witness and asked him if he knew Dr. Charles L. Dana as a medical writer. After an affirmative answer the witness was then asked: "I read from an article by Dr. Charles L. Dana on the subject of traumatic neurosis . . . what do you say to this?" (An excerpt was then read to the witness.) On appeal the court condemned that and similar questions, saying: "The plaintiff was thus enabled to bring to the knowledge of the jury the statement not under oath, of Dr. Charles L. Dana, whose writings on the subject of nervous diseases, the witness testified were considered authoritative by the medical profession, and without the defendant having an opportunity to cross examine Dr. Dana as to the facts and symptoms upon which he based his opinion, and as to whether perchance his views had undergone a change since the time the article was written." [7]

But when it comes to cross-examination a different rule applies. When an expert is being cross-examined, his qualifications as an expert may be tested in "any way which will enable the jury, who are to pass upon the weight to be given to his testimony, to judge intelligently about it. For that purpose it is perfectly proper to ask him whether or not the opinion he has expressed agrees with the opinion of other people who are conceded to be learned upon the same subject, because if an expert witness admitted that the opinion which he expressed was contrary to the opinion which was held upon the same subject by other men who were acquainted with the same science, it might unless the reasons which he gave for his opinion were satisfactory, tend strongly to detract from the weight which that opinion would otherwise receive. For the same reason, if the witness admitted that text writers of acknowledged authority had expressed opinions contrary to that one which he gave in regard to the matter under examination, that might go to detract from the weight to be given to such testimony. Therefore it has been the custom, in this state at least to call the attention of an expert witness, upon cross examination, to books upon the subject, and ask whether or not authors whom he admitted to be good authority had expressed opinions different from that which was given by him upon the stand. The reference to books in such cases is not made for the purpose

of making the statements in the books evidence before a jury, but solely for the purpose of ascertaining
the weight to be given to the testimony of the witness. The extent to which such examination may go
is very largely in the discretion of the court." [8]

CHAPTER XXI

THE DUTY OF A PHYSICIAN TO GIVE EXPERT TESTIMONY

EVERYONE within the jurisdiction of the court can be forced to lay aside whatever he is doing and to appear in court to testify. The process by which this is accomplished is a subpoena. Ordinarily this process is invoked where it is sought to have the witness testify as to some condition, act or occurrence which he has participated in, has seen or heard. But even if the purpose of the party in subpoenaing the witness is to endeavor to force him to give expert, as distinguished from lay testimony, the person subpoenaed must in either event respond to the subpoena and obey it. Not only must he come, but once upon the witness stand he must answer any question as to facts which the judge may allow, unless he asserts his constitutional privilege, that is, unless he declines to answer on the ground that it would tend to incriminate or degrade him. All of this is well known to everyone where the witness is produced to testify as to facts. But what of the witness who is brought to court to give expert testimony? He must come, but can he be forced to give expert testimony without being compensated for so doing, that is to say, must a man who has devoted his life to the study of a given subject and has become an expert in that field give the benefits of his knowledge and experience to any one who chooses to subpoena him? In other words, can he be deprived of his property (his knowledge and skill) without just compensation? There is no doubt that such a witness can be forced to come to court. A subpoena does not indicate whether the person subpoenaed is desired as a lay or as an expert witness. But once there, if he is put upon the stand and his expert opinion is asked, can he decline to give it unless and until he has been compensated? This question has been very definitely answered in New York.

In the Raizen case a physician,—an alienist—was subpoenaed as a witness and declined to give expert testimony. "There are," said the Appellate Division in upholding his position, "many authorities holding that an expert witness, that is, one possessing unusual skill and knowledge in a science, profession, or other calling, called upon to express an opinion based on conclusions derived not from personal knowledge of the facts of a given case, but from his ability to draw inferences and conclusions from reported facts, cannot be compelled to testify, in the absence of an agreement to do so for a stipulated compensation." [1] In a somewhat earlier case the same court declared, "It seems settled that if a medical witness, or other witness with technical qualifications, goes beyond mere testimony to facts, observed by the senses, and is asked to draw a technical inference or conclusion, he may properly stipulate for compensation." [2]

In another New York case it was stated: "It is the

theory of the law that everyone owes to the public, in the interest of justice, the duty of giving testimony as to facts within his personal knowledge.   This rule, however, does not go to the extent of obliging a person to give technical expert testimony without reasonable compensation.   The law regards such knowledge as the capital of the person possessing it which a litigant has no right to utilize without paying for it." [3] It would seem, however, from this case that the person giving expert testimony must claim compensation before he gives it, and that if he does not do so he waives his right to remuneration.   "It seems reasonable and should be the law," the court declared, "that, where one voluntarily testifies on request without insisting on compensation as a condition of giving his evidence, he should not afterward hold the person on whose behalf he testified to more than the statutory witness fee." [4]

The New York courts, however, have properly taken a strong position against agreements with expert witnesses, whereby the expert's compensation is to be made contingent upon the result of the litigation.   In one case a lawyer was disbarred who made an agreement with a doctor whereby the latter was to receive a substantial portion of the recovery if one were obtained. [5]

The New York rule, however, authorizing an expert witness to decline to give expert testimony in the absence of an agreement to do so for a stipulated compensation does not represent the prevailing view in the United States.   Indeed, "the weight of authority inclines to the view that an expert witness is not entitled to demand extra compensation before testifying to facts within his knowledge, although it may have required professional study, learning or skill to ascertain it." [6]

In an Alabama case a physician who declined to state the nature and character of the wound and its probable effect was fined for contempt of court. The fine was sustained upon appeal.[7]   In an Illinois case a doctor who was brought to court under an ordinary subpoena refused to answer a hypothetical question on the ground that as an expert witness he was entitled to a greater compensation than an ordinary witness, and that he was not required to give expert testimony without reasonable compensation. He was fined $25. for his refusal to testify and the fine was sustained upon appeal, where the court said that the requirement that he give expert testimony constituted no infringement on a property right.[8]

In a Massachusetts case a civil engineer was engaged six weeks before the trial to advise the defendant's attorney in regard to certain questions which were likely to arise. The agreement also provided that the expert would testify as such upon the trial. The engineer was subpoenaed as a witness, although he was not interrogated as to his opinion as an expert. He later sued for his compensation, and despite the defendant's contention that the promise to pay the expert was without consideration, the Supreme Court of Massachusetts held that the engineer was entitled to recover.   In a well considered opinion Judge Allen said: "We would be slow to admit that the court would be without power to require the attendance of a professional or skilled witness, upon a summons duly served, and with payment of the statutory fees, although he was unacquainted with the facts, and could testify only to opinions; but such power would hardly be exercised unless, in the opinion of the court, it was necessary for the purposes of justice. . . . Even in such case the court would probably be without the power to compel the witness to make a study of the case beforehand, or to pay attention to the body of evidence introduced by the parties with a view to forming an opinion thereon.   It would seem that one who is summoned as an expert would perform all that the court would require of him if he should hold himself in readiness to be called upon to testify to such opinion as he might have when his turn should come. . . .   If a party is content to rest upon his legal rights, and to summon the expert whose testimony he wishes to have, and to pay the statutory fees, without any previous engagement or understanding with him, and to take his chance of being able to get an attachment to bring the witness into court in case he should fail to appear, and if he thus succeeds in getting the testimony he wishes, and afterwards refuses to pay any special compensation, the question might be directly presented whether the witness would be entitled to recover anything on a quantum meruit. That question does not arise here." [9]

The text writers have strongly condemned the New York rule.   "It is not surprising," declares Mr. Chamberlayne in his Modern Law of Evidence, "to find that skilled witnesses whose services command high prices have objected to testifying unless suitably remunerated. Such a position, however, is distinctly anti-social. The common obligation upon all citizens to testify in aid of the ascertainment of truth is not to be evaded with any moral propriety. Courts in general have not hesitated to enforce this obligation in the case of an expert. His obligation, however, while it is the same as that of other witnesses, is no greater. . . . If, however, he is expected to spend time in making researches or otherwise perfecting himself to aid the court or jury he may properly demand that he be first compensated in some reasonable way for so doing." [10]

Professor Wigmore declares that the argument that expert witnesses should not be compelled to give expert testimony without compensation is "specious." "The hardship," he says, "upon the professional man who loses his days' fees of fifty or one hundred dollars is not greater relatively than upon the storekeeper or the mechanic who loses his day's earnings of two dollars or ten dollars. . . ." [11]

The New York rule, in my opinion, is more just than that obtaining in other states, nor can I find myself in accord with Professor Wigmore that the argument supporting it is "specious." There is a vast difference between a professional man being forced to give expert testimony and the requirement that a storekeeper leave his store and testify as to some facts within his knowledge. It is true that both the storekeeper and the physician are required to leave their regular employment for the day, but the storekeeper

is not required to donate any of his merchandise or
stock of goods, whereas the physician, if required to
give expert testimony, must surrender his property,
namely, his store of knowledge which it has required
much capital to acquire.   The physician has as much
right to be compensated for his store of goods,
namely, his knowledge, as has the grocer for his cans
of tomatoes or his green vegetables on his shelves.
If the physician is merely compelled to testify as to a
fact then Professor Wigmore's argument is sound.
In such case his position is exactly similar to that of
the storekeeper.   But when the physician is required
to give, without compensation, of his store of goods,
namely, his knowledge, all similarity between his position and that of the storekeeper ceases.   To make
the two cases analogous would necessitate the requirement that the storekeeper, in addition to losing
his day's time, be compelled likewise to donate some
part of his merchandise.   Such a requirement would
obviously work a deprivation of the storekeeper's
property, without due process of law.   But if this is
true of the storekeeper, it is equally true of the physician.   To require a physician to render expert testimony without proper compensation would, in the
last analysis, be anti-social.   Outstanding men in the
profession would be constantly subpoenaed to give
gratuitous expert opinions.   This would mean not
only a loss of time and a loss of revenue for themselves, but it would compel them to cut short, or at
least to curtail the time they devote to the treatment
and care of charity patients.

PART VI

THE DOCTOR ON THE WITNESS STAND

CHAPTER XXII

THE SELECTION OF A WITNESS

WHERE a lawyer is confronted with establishing the facts he naturally has little choice in the witnesses whom he will call. Those who saw, or heard, or did, necessarily must be the witnesses to testify concerning the things of which they have personal first hand knowledge. They may be intelligent or stupid, they may have good eye-sight and hearing, or they may have bad, their memories may be retentive or faulty, they may have good characters or they may have bad, they may be honest or they may be dishonest, their records may be unblemished or they may have been convicted of crime, their characters and their personalities may be winning or they may be repellent, their manner of testifying may carry conviction in the jury's mind or it may be so hesitating as to cause suspicion, even where they are telling the truth. No lawyer can control these things, nor can he even predict in advance what impression his prospective witnesses will make. Sometimes a man of seeming stalwart strength and courage, will become a weakling in the hands of cross examining counsel, whereas a fragile woman will display an iron nerve. A thoroughly educated person may appear stupid, and an illiterate may display a quick and keen intelligence. Every

trial lawyer has had these experiences.   One of the
many worries that he carries into the court room with
him is as to how his witness will "stand up," and he is
often destined to both pleasant and unpleasant sur-
prises.

Yet despite these uncertainties, there are certain
qualities which every lawyer knows are apt to make
a man a good witness, if he possesses them.   These
might thus be enumerated in the order of their importance: First, honesty; second, good character and
reputation; third, quick intelligence and attentive
ears; fourth, courage,—the determination not to be
browbeaten from what he knows to be the truth; fifth,
good personality and a presentable personal appearance; sixth, good manners and tact; seventh, terse-
ness,—(the quality of answering briefly and of not
volunteering).   While the possession of all these
qualities will not guarantee that their possessor will
be a satisfactory witness, a lawyer calling him will do
so with a feeling of much confidence.

Where, therefore, a lawyer has the right of selec-
tion,—as in the case of expert witnesses—he should
make his choice from those who possess the foregoing
traits rather than from those who do not possess
them.   It goes without saying that he should select
an expert who is not only well read, but who has had
actual personal experience in treating the particular
malady which is involved in the litigation.   Ofttimes
he will have a wealth of witnesses to choose from.
In making his decision he should be guided by his
estimate of the witness possessing the traits above

enumerated, rather than by the importunities of his client or the zeal of the expert who is volunteering. It is good judgment to select the best one and to stop there.   The more the witnesses the greater the opportunities for disaster.   The lawyer's technique in choosing the expert witnesses whom he will call determines, ofttimes, the outcome of the trial.   I remember well in one of the first malpractice cases I tried the first expert whom I called had made an excellent impression.   When he left the stand I felt that the case was won.   We adjourned at that point for the luncheon recess, during which my client expatiated upon the merits of one of his professional brethren,—a "professor."   He wanted me to call him.   I argued against it, but he insisted upon it. Mistakenly I yielded.   I called the "professor" when we returned to court.   He went all to pieces on the stand and I almost lost the case.   But I learned my lesson.

CHAPTER XXIII

THE WORK OF TESTIFYING

UNLESS it be personal participation in armed conflict, there is no severer testing ground of a man's character than the witness stand. It is in every sense an ordeal. It requires everything a man has in coolness, intelligence, memory and courage. The witness is alone. Not only is he alone, but he is engaging in a single-handed and unequal contest. He is circumscribed by definite limitations. He cannot argue, it is not his to reason why, but to answer,—always to answer the questions. He is not engaged in a debate, he is not there to deliver an oration, he is there for the one and sole purpose of answering questions. In an atmosphere surcharged with tension his nerve must not snap, under provocation he must not lose his temper, when met with marked discourtesy he must remain polite, under attack he must keep cool. He is the centre of all eyes in the court room, he is especially the cynosure of the twelve pairs of eyes in the jury box. His every word, inflexion, mannerism, even the way he moistens his lips or asks for a drink of water is under the surveillance of the most attentive of all audiences. Everything he does as well as says is watched, measured, weighed and judged. His whole self is in the crucible. Strong men have wilted under this ordeal, egoists have been deflated, braggarts have been written down, tricksters have been exposed, and liars have been caught redhanded in their perjury. It is well then that one who is about to mount the witness stand should consider seriously the nature of the task he is about to assume.

The art of giving testimony, like all arts is good in proportion to its artlessness. Like all arts it is not mere compliance with set rules or formulae. The art of giving testimony is the art of being one's honest self and of persuading those who hear him that he is worthy of belief. Good witnesses like good artists are not always those with the best formal education. College graduates ofttimes have revealed themselves as dull and slow, men of no schooling frequently appear as keen and alert thinkers, capable not infrequently of unhorsing the most vigorous and adroit of cross examiners. What then is the prospective witness to do? Is the ordeal which he is about to undergo, one against which he can do nothing to prepare? Not with any hope that I have fully covered the ground, but with a feeling that my long experience with courts and juries might have evoked some useful suggestions, I once wrote an editorial for the New York State Journal of Medicine on this subject. I shall here condense and with some improvements repeat what many of you read in that editorial.

First: *Tell the truth.* Tell the truth, the whole truth and nothing but the truth. You will take an oath to do this. You will be under an obligation to

yourself as well as to your God to do so.   Deliberate
false swearing with respect to a material matter is
punishable by a long term in state's prison.   There
are fewer prosecutions for perjury than there should
be, but the possibility of an indictment hangs over the
head of every perjurer.   One who contemplates lying
under oath is embarking on a hazardous journey.
The probabilities of detection are great.   Truth like
beauty is a thing that is perceived and sensed and felt.
There is a look about a man who tells the truth that
is unmistakable.   The same is true of him who bears
false witness.   The truth is perceived and sensed and
felt, but also it is capable at times of mathematical
demonstration.   Not only is there the strongest
moral and legal obligation to give truthful testimony,
but the party who becomes a witness (and usually he
does) should not forget that one little lie, if exposed,
will lose him every vestige of the jury's confidence.
Jurors heed and follow the court's injunction: "If you
believe that any witness wilfully testified falsely in
regard to a material matter you may disregard his entire testimony."

Second: *Come prepared*.   Refresh your recollection as to the names, persons, places, figures and dates
about which you will probably be asked.   If you keep
books or diaries, go over them carefully to check and
recheck your memory.   Bring them with you to court
so that you may use them there if permitted to refresh
your recollection.   If you are to give expert testimony, it is well to go over carefully the text books
and the literature concerning the subject about which

you will be asked, to the end that you will not be easily tripped by the smart cross examiner. No surgeon endeavors to remember the exact names or locations of every infinitesimal nerve or blood vessel, any more than a judge or lawyer carries in his mind the provisions of every statute or decision, but jurors do not realize this, and therefore, even the most competent man may be discomfited by some unusual question about anatomy or pathology.

Third: *Do not be afraid.* The honest witness need not fear. Look the lawyer squarely in the eye. Look also into the eyes of as many jurors as you can. If the judge asks a question, turn and look him squarely in the eye and give your answer. No one loves a coward. Remember that it is not only your story, but you, that is being judged. Do not permit yourself to be spiritually browbeaten, nor forced into an admission that the facts do not require you to make. Sit there with head erect, be yourself and fear no man.

Fourth: *Be natural.* Do not "talk down" to the jury, neither should you fawn before the judge. Do not under dress or over dress for the occasion. Be your normal natural self as you are in your everyday life. If you are just an ordinary fellow like the rest of us, do not assume an intellectual monocle or ape the manners of a grand duke. Do not use long or Latin words so as to impress. If such a word is necessary quickly translate or explain it before you go on.

Fifth: *Be modest.* Nothing is more impressive than modesty. If you are an outstanding character the fact will soon enough reveal itself. Do not exaggerate your qualifications, your capacity or your experience.

Sixth: *Be frank.* Do not hesitate to admit a fact because you think it hurts you. Usually there are in every case some facts which your counsel might wish otherwise. The best way to meet them is with candor and frankness. Candor is a great disinfectant.

Seventh: *Be attentive to questions.* Listen carefully before you answer the question,—be sure you have heard it and have understood it. You cannot understand a question unless you listen to it. If after you have listened carefully to the question, you still do not understand it, do not be afraid to say so. No judge will force a witness to answer a question which he cannot honestly understand.

Eighth: *Do not volunteer.* You are not called upon to make a speech, your only duty is to answer questions. A volunteered answer usually leads to trouble, often to disaster.

Ninth: *Do not attempt to be an advocate.* Your duty, if you are a lay witness, is to give the court the facts, not to argue about them or to draw conclusions from them. If you are called as an expert, while you may have a wide latitude, make your opinions scientifically correct, but present them as a scientist rather than an advocate. As a witness let your eloquence be that of truth alone. Leave advocacy to counsel. Presumably, he will perform it well, if not, you cannot help him from the witness stand by departing from the rôle of witness.

Tenth: *Do not lose your temper.*   Insulting questions, or those with insulting innuendoes will sometimes be allowed.   Ignore the insult in the question and conserve your mental resources for answering it. A calm and dispassionate answer to such a question will win you friends and sympathy in the jury box.

Eleventh: *Be courteous.*   No matter how absurd the question, answer it without facetiousness.   The folly of a question will be more easily exposed by a serious answer than through any manifestation of your appreciation of the ignorance or shortcomings of the questioner.   The witness stand is not a good place for the smart aleck.

Twelfth: *Keep your voice up.*   Your testimony will be of no value unless it has been heard.   The occupants of our courtrooms in the large cities are accustomed to compete with passing trucks, brass bands and riveting machines.   If to this annoyance there is added the strain of endeavoring to catch what a mumbling witness says, the tried tempers of the judge, the jury and the lawyers will not render your stay, however brief upon the witness stand, more pleasant.   Moreover, a witness (especially one belonging to the male sex) if he will not talk up, will probably be put down as one who is whispering a false answer which he does not dare to speak out loud.

PART VII

THE DOCTOR AND THE CRIMINAL LAW

CHAPTER XXIV

ASSAULT

IT would be well for every citizen to have some knowledge of the criminal law, it is particularly important for surgeons and physicians. They deal with life and limb and health, with poisons, instruments and anaesthesias. To know in what way the criminal law takes cognizance of these things should be useful to the members of the medical profession. There is an old maxim that ignorance of the law excuses no man.

We have previously pointed out that to operate upon a person without his consent is an assault. It gives rise to a civil action, but it also may be ground for a criminal prosecution.[1] While I have found no instance in which a doctor has been prosecuted criminally for assault, and such a case, except if occasioned by exaggerated circumstances, is not likely to occur, still we should take brief note of this possible offense in passing.

CHAPTER XXV

ABORTION

THE crime of abortion should be carefully considered. "A person who, with intent thereby to procure the miscarriage of a woman," declares the New York Penal Law, "unless the same is necessary to preserve the life of the woman, or of the child with which she is pregnant, either: 1. Prescribes, supplies, or administers to a woman, *whether pregnant or not,* or advises or causes a woman to take any medicine, drug, or substance; or, 2. Uses, or causes to be used, any instrument or other means, is guilty of abortion, and is punishable by imprisonment in a state prison for not more than four years, or in a county jail for not more than one year." [1]

In every crime two elements must coexist: first, a criminal intent, and second, some overt act done in furtherance of that intent. In abortion the required criminal intent is the intent "to produce the miscarriage of a woman unless the same is necessary to preserve the life of the woman, or of the child with which she is pregnant." The intent alone (however interdicted in the domain of ethics) is not sufficient to constitute the crime; something must be done to carry that intent into effect. Thus, in the Phelps case, the defendant was indicted for advising a pregnant

woman to take drug to bring on a miscarriage. The
advice was not acted upon and so the conviction was
reversed. "For a man to be 'guilty of abortion' who
has advised the woman to take a drug," declared the
New York Court of Appeals, "it is necessarily and
logically to be implied that his advice shall have been
followed by the act. Otherwise we should have to
draw the apparently absurd conclusion that the legislature intended that abortion could be committed, or
caused, by the act of offering advice." [2]

Let not the criminally minded, however, if there be
any such left in the profession, take too much com-
fort from the Phelps case, for the court there called
attention to the fact that the defendant "was accused
of the crime of abortion, not of an attempt to commit
the crime." The suggestion is thereby clearly left
that had the indictment charged an attempt instead
of a completed crime, that the conviction might have
been affirmed, despite the fact that the patient did not
take the drug. For a person who "unlawfully attempts to commit a crime," is as guilty as one who
achieves success, although the punishment is less. [3]
The legal definition of this offense is "an act done with
intent to commit a crime, and tending but failing to
effect its commission." [4] In criminal attempts the
crime depends upon the mind and intent of the wrong-
doer and not upon the result of that attempt. [5] "An
attempt is made when an opportunity occurs and the
intending perpetrator has done some act tending to
accomplish his purpose, although he is baffled by an
unexpected obstacle or condition." [6] Thus, where a

doctor laid out his instruments and otherwise prepared for the operation, but was arrested before he actually performed it, his conviction of the crime of attempting to commit the crime of abortion was affirmed.[7]

From the statutory definition of abortion we must observe that if the miscarriage of a woman is necessary to preserve her life, or that of the child with which she is pregnant, the procuring of the miscarriage is not a crime. It is, however, not necessary for the district attorney to establish that the miscarriage was not necessary to preserve either of these two lives, it is for the accused who asserts that it was, to prove it.[8] But, declared the court in one case, "it is not at all likely that courts in the administration of justice would require more, in explanation of the operation performed, to overcome the existing penalty than that an honest judgment was exercised declaring the necessity of resorting to an instrument for the purpose of relieving the mother or saving the child." [9] For those with inclination to pursue this branch of the subject further, I would commend a full reading of the opinion in the Hammer case,[10] in which the jury as well as the Appellate Court were able to discern that the doctor's defense was a mere subterfuge.

In many states the crime of abortion does not depend upon the actual pregnancy of the woman. In California,[11] New Jersey [12] and Maryland,[13] the woman must be pregnant. In Connecticut,[14] Massachusetts,[15] Minnesota [16] and Pennsylvania [17] the fact of pregnancy is not an essential ingredient of the crime. In New York the supplying of medicine or drugs with intent to procure a miscarriage constitutes the crime whether the woman is "pregnant or not." Where, however, an instrument is used for that purpose, it would seem that the woman must be pregnant.[18] But even in those states where the proof of pregnancy is essential, it is sufficient for the prosecution to establish those symptoms and conditions which indicate to a medical man that pregnancy exists.[19] Absolute knowledge of pregnancy is not required. "If there be a mere suspicion that pregnancy exists there may be an intent to cause a miscarriage if the suspected condition is in existence." [20]

We have previously remarked that criminal intent is an essential ingredient of a crime. This may be established as an inference from all the circumstances of the case. Perhaps it might act as an additional deterrent upon those (if there are any left) who contemplate embarking on a career of abortion, to learn that proof of the performance of "former similar criminal abortions on the same or another woman is admissible under the authorities to prove such specific intent." [21] Such proof need not be confined to former convictions; it "may be made by parol evidence and where defendant was never tried for such offenses." [22] The medical man, therefore, who strays from the legitimate practice of his profession into the criminal by-paths, in addition to the loss of all decency and self-respect, incurs a sufficient danger of penal serviture if he strays but once; he immeasurably multiplies his chance of punishment if he forms the habit.

In most jurisdictions the "administration of drugs or use of instruments with intent to procure abortion" is a crime "although no abortion is actually produced and although the female survives the operation." [23] In Ohio, however, no crime has been committed by the administration of drugs or the use of instruments with intent to procure a miscarriage "unless it results either in abortion or death." [24]

In several of the states where death results from a criminal abortion the perpetrator is guilty of manslaughter. Thus, in New York, the statute reads: "A person who provides, supplies, or administers to a woman, whether pregnant or not, or who prescribes for, or advises or procures a woman to take any medicine, drug, or substance, or who uses or employs, or causes to be used or employed, any instrument or other means, with intent thereby to procure the miscarriage of a woman, unless the same is necessary to preserve her life, in case the death of the woman or of any quick child of which she is pregnant, is thereby produced, is guilty of manslaughter in the first degree." [25] This offense is punishable by a term not exceeding twenty years.[26] In this offense as in abortion, if the defense is that the abortion was necessary to save the life of the patient, this must be established by the accused. The prosecution is not bound to prove the negative.[27]

CHAPTER XXVI

CONTRACEPTION

BEFORE leaving this important, but unpleasant subject, we should take note of the statutes affecting contraception.   Birth control is now a topic much de-
bated.   It has strong protagonists, and opponents
equally in earnest.   We shall not here in any way
enter the lists.   The debate would be quite useless to
those who seek knowledge as to what the law is, not
what some persons think it should be.   In most of
the states the selling or giving away of any instrument, drug, article or medicine for the prevention of
contraception, or the giving of information stating
when, where and how such instruments or articles
can be obtained, is made a criminal offense.[1]   The
laws differ, of course, somewhat in the several states,
but most of them are similar to the New York statute,
which provides that "a person who sells, lends, gives
away, or in any manner exhibits or offers to sell, lend
or give away, or has in his possession with intent to
sell, lend or give away, or advertises, or offers for
sale, loan or distribution, any instrument or article,
or any recipe, drug or medicine for the prevention of
conception, or for causing unlawful abortion, or purporting to be for the prevention of conception, or for
causing unlawful abortion, or advertises, or holds out

187

representations that it can be so used or applied, or any such description as will be calculated to lead another to so use or apply any such article, recipe, drug, medicine or instrument, or who writes or prints, or causes to be written or printed, a card, circular, pamphlet, advertisement or notice of any kind, or gives information orally, stating when, where, how, of whom, or by what means such an instrument, article, recipe, drug or medicine can be purchased or obtained, or who manufactures any such instrument, article, recipe, drug or medicine," is guilty of a misdemeanor, and shall be sentenced to not less than ten days, nor more than one year's imprisonment, or be fined not less than fifty dollars, nor more than one thousand dollars or both fine and imprisonment for each offense.[2]

This law has been in force since 1887; it has been declared constitutional.[3]   "It was proper for the legislature," the court in one case said, "to determine whether the general dissemination of information upon the subject of birth control and the sale of articles designed to prevent conception were prejudicial to public morals and inimical to the welfare and interests of the community." [4]

Perhaps one of the most celebrated prosecutions under this section was that of People vs. Sanger. The defendant was there convicted and her conviction was affirmed. She contended that the statute was broad enough to prevent a duly licensed physician from giving advice and help to his married patients in a proper case, and that hence the law was unconsti-

tutional.   But the Court of Appeals overruled this
contention, referring to section 1145 of the Penal
Law, which expressly excepts from the prohibition of
the contraception statute "an article or instrument
used or applied by a physician lawfully practicing or
by their direction or prescription for the cure or prevention of disease."   This exception in behalf of
physicians, the court said, "does not permit adver-
tisements regarding such matters nor promiscuous advice to patients irrespective of their condition, but it
is broad enough to protect the physician who in good
faith gives such help or advice to a married person to
cure or prevent disease." [5]   Mrs. Sanger's other
points were briefly disposed of by the court in these
words: "Much of the argument presented to us by
the appellant touching social conditions and socio-
logical questions are matters for the legislature and
not for the courts." [6]

CHAPTER XXVII

NARCOTICS

It is not only to the statutes of the several states, but to the laws of Congress that the physician must turn in order to discover the full extent of the increasingly prevalent attempts to regulate the conduct of the individual by means of criminal enactments. The criminal law in this country embraces now a field undreamed of by the founders of the government. One of the Federal statutes providing fines and imprisonment is the so-called Harrison Narcotic Law.[1]

A person who violates the act may be fined not more than $2,000. or be imprisoned not more than five years or both in the discretion of the court.[2]   Physicians (if registered with the collector) may dispense such drugs to persons whom they "personally attend" in the course of their professional practice.   Where such drugs are dispensed to a patient not personally attended by the physician, he must keep a record showing the amount dispensed together with the date and the name and address of the patient.[3]

If a physician intends to dispense narcotics, he must register with the Collector of Internal Revenue of his district, his name and place of business, for which registration he must pay an annual tax of one dollar.[4] All persons not registered are not only forbidden to sell, but to have in their possession the prohibited drugs.[5] But this prohibition does not apply to employees or nurses of registered physicians "having possession or control by virtue" of their employment or occupation, and not on their "own account." [6] Nor does it apply to the possession of any such narcotics as have "been prescribed in good faith by a physician." [7]

Throughout the law the purpose is apparent to prohibit the illicit trade in narcotics, not to interfere with the legitimate practice of medicine. Thus, in the same section which prohibits the sale of narcotics except in the original stamped packages, there is a proviso that this shall "not apply to any person having in his or her possession any of the aforesaid drugs which have been obtained from a registered dealer in pursuance of a prescription written for legitimate uses issued by a physician," nor does it apply to "the dispensing or administration or giving away of any of the aforesaid drugs to a patient by a registered physician . . . in the course of his professional practice and where said drugs are dispensed or administered to the patient for legitimate medical purposes and the record kept as required by this act." [8]

Throughout the regulations adopted by the Commissioner of Internal Revenue the same intent is noticeable. Thus, it is there provided that a "duly qualified practitioner is not required to pay additional tax on account of the sale of narcotics or drugs for legitimate medical purposes to his own bonafide patients." [9] And again: "A prescription for narcotic drugs may be issued only by a physician, dentist, veterinary surgeon, or other practitioner who has duly registered. . . ." [10]   And still further: "A prescription, in order to be effective in legalizing the possession of unstamped narcotic drugs and eliminating the necessity for use of order forms, must be issued for legitimate medical purposes." [11]   The purpose of the Harrison Narcotic Law, the United States Supreme Court has said, is "to confine the distribution of these drugs to the regular and lawful course of professional practice, and that not everything called a prescription is necessarily such." [12]   The same authority has said that the "declared object of the Narcotic Law is to provide revenue, and . . . whatever additional moral end it may have in view must 'be reached only through the revenue measure.' . . . Obviously, direct control of medical practice in the states is beyond the power of the Federal government.   Incidental regulation of such practice by Congress through a taxing act cannot extend to matters plainly inappropriate and unnecessary to reasonable enforcement of a revenue measure.   The enactment levies a tax . . . and may regulate medical practice in the states only so far as reasonably appropriate for or merely incidental to its enforcement." [13]

The character and purpose of the law has given rise to much judicial controversy as to whether a physician may lawfully prescribe morphine to an addict in sufficient quantities merely to keep him comfortable. [14]   This question has now been definitely settled by the Linder case, where a physician was indicted

for having knowingly sold to one Ida Casey one tab-
let of morphine without her written order on the
form issued by the Commissioner of Internal Revenue.   The indictment charged that the patient (for
such she was) did not require the administration of
either morphine or cocaine by reason of any disease,
other than addiction.   The regulations at that time
declared that "an order purporting to be a prescription issued to an addict or habitual user of narcotics
not in the course of professional treatment in an attempted cure of the habit, but for the purpose of
providing the user with narcotics sufficient to keep
him comfortable is not a prescription within the
meaning of the act." [15]   The defendant was convicted.   His conviction was affirmed by the Circuit
Court of Appeals, but the Supreme Court reversed it.
The court called attention to the fact that it was the
regulation and not the statute which prohibited the
dispensing to an addict, and that the regulation could
not enlarge the statute.   The statute "says nothing
of 'addicts' and does not undertake to prescribe methods for their medical treatment.   They are diseased
and proper subjects for such treatment, and we cannot properly conclude that a physician acted improperly or unwisely or for other than medical purposes,
solely because he has dispensed to one and in ordinary
good faith, four small tablets of morphine or cocaine
for relief of conditions incident to addiction." [16]

Of course, the drug must be administered in good
faith and in the course of professional practice.
"What constitutes bona fide medical practice," said

the court, "must be determined upon consideration of evidence and attending circumstances. Mere pretense of such practice of course cannot legalize forbidden sales or otherwise nullify valid provisions of the statute, or defeat such regulations as may be fairly appropriate to its enforcement within the proper limitation of a revenue measure. . . . Manifestly the phrase 'to a patient' and 'in the course of his professional practice only' are intended to confine the immunity of a registered physician, in dispensing the narcotic drugs mentioned in the act strictly within the appropriate bounds of a physician's professional practice, and not to extend it to include a sale to a dealer or a distribution intended to cater to the appetite or satisfy the craving of one addicted to the use of the drug. A 'prescription' issued for either of the latter purposes protects not the physician who issues it nor the dealer who knowingly accepts and fills it." [17]

Turning to the indictment, Mr. Justice McReynolds, speaking for an unanimous court, did "not question the doctor's good faith nor the wisdom or propriety of his action according to medical standards. It does not allege that he dispensed the drug otherwise than to a patient in the course of his professional practice or for other than medical purposes. The facts disclosed no conscious design to violate the law, no cause to suspect that the recipient intended to sell or otherwise dispose of the drugs and no real probability that she would not consume them." [18] The mere fact that a doctor's patient may be a drug addict does not render the doctor's act unlawful solely because he has dispensed a small amount of morphine or cocaine for the "relief of conditions incident to addiction." [19]

While a sharp distinction was drawn between a case where a doctor administers a narcotic in good faith in pursuance of a bona fide medical practice and one where the doctor merely uses his position to engage in the general distribution of narcotics to those who are in no way his patients, the court said that there was no authority "for holding that a physician who acts bona fide and according to fair medical standards may never give an addict moderate amounts of drugs for self administration in order to relieve conditions incident to addiction. Enforcement of the tax demands no such drastic rule, and if the act had such scope it would certainly encounter grave constitutional difficulties." [20]

As further evidence of the intent of the law to protect physicians in their bona fide practice, the present regulations provide that "in the treatment of incurable disease, such as cancer, advanced tuberculosis, and other diseases well recognized as coming within this class, where the physician directly in charge of a bona fide patient suffering from such disease prescribes for such patient, in the course of his professional practice and strictly for legitimate medical purposes, and in so prescribing endorses upon the prescription that the drug is dispensed in the treatment of an incurable disease; or if he prefers he may endorse upon the prescription 'Exception (1), article

85,' " will not be regarded as guilty of a violation of the law.[21]   The same article provides that "an order purporting to be a prescription issued to an addict or habitual user of narcotics, not in the course of professional treatment but for the purpose of providing the user with narcotics sufficient to keep him comfortable by maintaining his customary use, is not a prescription within the meaning and intent of the act; and the person filling and receiving drugs under such an order, as well as the person issuing it, may be regarded as guilty of violation of the law."   And the article continues: "A physician may prescribe for an aged and infirm addict whose collapse would result from the withdrawal of the drug, provided he endorses upon the prescription that the patient is aged and infirm, giving age; or if he prefers he may endorse upon the prescription 'Exception (2), article 85.' " [22]

The rather anomalous character of the Harrison Narcotic Act, in that it is a combined tax and criminal measure, is shown from one of the regulations which provides that the "Commissioner of Prohibition, with the advice and consent of the secretary of the Treasury has authority to compromise any civil or criminal cases arising under this act instead of commencing suit thereon; and, with the advice and consent of the said Secretary and the recommendation of the Attorney-General, he may compromise any such case after suit thereon has been commenced." [23]

Any physician who makes a practice of prescribing narcotic drugs should acquaint himself very carefully with all of the provisions of the Harrison Narcotic

Law and the regulations adopted by the Commissioner of Internal Revenue, and in case of doubt
should consult counsel before acting. He should
likewise be familiar with the particular provisions of
the statutes in his own state as there are many state
enactments on this subject.[24]

CHAPTER XXVIII

PRESCRIPTION OF LIQUOR

WE shall now make brief reference to a rather hackneyed subject,—the National Prohibition Act.[1] The act declares that "no one but a physician holding a permit to prescribe liquor shall issue any prescription for liquor. And no physician shall prescribe liquor unless after careful physical examination of the person for whose use such prescription is sought, or if such examination is found impracticable, then upon the best information obtainable, he in good faith believes that the use of such liquor as a medicine by such person is necessary and will afford relief to him from such known ailment. *Not more than a pint of spirituous liquor to be taken internally shall be prescribed for use by the same person within any period of ten days and no prescription shall be filled more than once......"* [2]

In 1922, Dr. Samuel W. Lambert of New York, applied for an injunction to restrain Yellowley, the acting prohibition director, and other officials, "from interfering with complainant in his acts as a physician in prescribing vinous or spirituous liquors . . . for medicinal purposes." Dr. Lambert in his bill of complaint stated that in certain cases, including some subject to his professional advice, "the use of spirituous liquor internally as a medicine in an amount exceeding one pint in ten days is necessary for the proper treatment of patients in order to afford relief from human ailments;" and further that he did not "intend to prescribe the use of liquor for beverage purposes." He alleged further that "to treat the diseases of his patients and to promote their physical well-being, according to the untrammelled exercise of his best skill and scientifically trained judgment, and, to that end, to advise the use of such medicine and medical treatment as in his opinion are best calculated to effect their cure and establish their health, is an essential part of his constitutional rights as a physician."   The United States Supreme Court divided five to four upon this question in deciding against Dr. Lambert's contentions.   The court held that this limitation upon the professional practice of a physician was constitutional.

One of the strongest dissenting opinions ever written by the Supreme Court was filed by Mr. Justice Sutherland in which three of his associates concurred. Speaking for the minority he declared: "By the legislation now under review, the authority of Congress is so exercised that the reserved power of the States to control the practice of medicine is directly invaded, to the illegitimate end that the prescription and use of liquors for medicinal purposes is prohibited. . . . The effect of upholding the legislation is to deprive the States of the exclusive power, which the Eighteenth Amendment has not destroyed, of controlling

medical practice and transfer it in part to Congress." [3]
The dissenting opinion is an interesting one, but it is
no protection to those who do not comply with the
statute which was upheld by a majority of the court.

CHAPTER XXIX

PRACTICING WHILE INTOXICATED

BEFORE leaving the subject of criminal law applicable to the practice of medicine, we should call attention to a New York statute which should be read and pondered, although so far as I can find, no prosecution has ever been instituted under it. This statute declares that "a physician or surgeon, or person practicing as such, who, being in a state of intoxication, without a design to effect death, administers a poisonous drug or medicine, or does any other act as a physician or surgeon, to another person, which produces the death of the latter, is guilty of manslaughter in the second degree." [1] This offense is punishable by a term not exceeding fifteen years, or by a fine of not more than one thousand dollars, or by both.[2] Where a physician while intoxicated does any act to another person "by which the life of the latter is endangered or his health seriously affected," he is guilty of a misdemeanor [3] punishable by imprisonment in a penitentiary or county jail for not more than one year or by a fine of not more than five hundred dollars.[4]

CHAPTER XXX

FALSE CERTIFICATES OF HEALTH

IN closing this brief discussion of the criminal law as it applies to doctors, we should call attention to a New York Statute which provides that "a physician who knowingly gives a false certificate, or makes a false representation, for the purpose of enabling or assisting a person, to be discharged, excused or exempted from service, as a trial juror in the city and county of New York, or in the county of Kings is guilty of a misdemeanor." [1]   This quotation should be pondered by those doctors, if there are any, who have a tendency to too great a liberality in certifying to bad health.   If any one asks why such a false certificate is a crime in the counties of New York and Kings, but not in Albany or Onondaga, my only answer is that the law, especially statute law, like other serious subjects, has its occasional whimsicalities.

CONCLUSION

CONCLUSION

IN the foregoing pages I have attempted to set down those essential principles of law which govern and affect the doctor in his work. Taking a leaf from the pages of preventive medicine, I have tried to explain the nature of a malpractice action, in the hope that an understanding of this malady may render those who understand it more immune to its dread ravages. Having had so long and so congenial an acquaintance with the medical profession, I should like to close this book with some words of larger scope than the mere catalog of suggestions how to avoid a law suit.

In this time of revolutionary change, this era of shifting standards, it would be well occasionally to recall the things which are not altered by the years. It would be well to remember that more important even than science is character. Character is the real basis of true professional attainment. Without character a doctor is a menace to his fellow men. The greater his intellectual endowment, the wider his experience, the more agile his facility, the more dangerous he is. All professions of late years have been debilitated by the influx of some men who never should be trusted with a patient or a client. The professions of medicine and of the law, if they would survive in public confidence and usefulness, must

purge themselves of such members and must keep
constantly on guard against the admission of such
men.   The recent work of the New York Bar Asso-
ciations and of the Medical Society of the State of
New York have done much in this direction.   Similar
efforts in other parts of the country would be equally
productive of good results.   But perhaps such efforts
would be unnecessary if the words of wise counsel of
the sages of the profession were more generally
heeded.

Thirty-seven years ago there died in Cambridge,
Massachusetts, a gentleman of the old school.   He
was a poet, a scholar and a physician.   His essay on
the Contagiousness of Puerperal Fever published
when he was but thirty-four, entitles him to the rank
of scientist.   Not only was Dr. Oliver Wendell
Holmes a scientist, he was a reformer; his insistence
that the unclean hands of physicians were responsible
for much of the infant mortality brought him the
"virulent opposition" of the reactionaries of his day,
but it has brought man also the assent and the approval of posterity.[1]   His paper on Puerperal Infection will be found among his medical essays, which
should, I think, be part of the required reading of
every medical student.   Not only are they of vital
interest to the profession, but their crisp and pungent
style, make them for the layman as fascinating as his
"Elsie Venner," and the "Autocrat of the Breakfast
Table."   In his Valedictory Address delivered to the
graduating class of the Bellevue Hospital College
more than sixty years ago will be found advice as

timely now as when it was uttered. "Book knowledge, lecture knowledge, examination knowledge," Dr. Holmes said, "are all in the brain. But work knowledge is not only in the brain, it is in the senses, in the muscles, in the ganglia of the sympathetic nerves. . . . See a skillful surgeon handle a broken limb; see a wise old physician smile away a case that looks to the novice as if the sexton would be sent for; mark what a large experience has done for those who were fitted to profit by it, and you will feel convinced that much as you know, something is still left for you to learn. . . . The young man knows the rules, but the old man knows the exceptions. . . . The young man feels uneasy if he is not continually doing something to stir up his patients' internal arrangements. The old man takes things more quietly and is much more willing to let well enough alone." [2]

Then, as though fearing that he might be charged with holding a brief for age, the Massachusetts sage declared of the young man: "His education in all the accessory branches is more recent, and therefore nearer the existing condition of knowledge. He finds it easier than his seniors to accept the improvements which every year is bringing forward. New ideas build their nests in young men's brains. 'Revolutions are not made by men in spectacles' . . . and the first whispers of a new truth are not caught by those who begin to feel the need of an ear trumpet. Granting all those advantages to the young man, he ought, nevertheless, to go on improving, on the whole as a medical practitioner, with every year, until he has ripened into a well mellowed maturity.   But to improve he must be good for something at the start. If you ship a poor cask of wine to India and back, if you keep it half a century, it only grows thinner and sharper." [3]

At the very outset of his address Dr. Holmes stated the question which must force itself on every young practitioner: "How am I to obtain patients and to keep their confidence?" [4]   His whole address was really directed to the answering of that question. At one point he said: "To get business a man must really want it; and do you suppose that when you are in the middle of a heated caucus, or half way through a delicate analysis, or in the spasm of an unfinished ode, your eyes rolling in a fine frenzy of poetical composition, you want to be called to a teething infant, or an ancient person groaning under the griefs of a lumbago?   I think I know more than one young man whose doctor's sign proclaimed his readiness to serve mankind in that capacity, but who hated the sound of a patient's knock. . . .   The community soon finds out whether you are in earnest and really mean business, or whether you are one of those diplomaed dilettanti who like the amusement of quasi medical studies, but have no idea of wasting their precious time in putting their knowledge in practice for the benefit of their suffering fellow creatures." [5]

The father of the future Supreme Court Justice then stressed the importance of getting along with our fellow men.   "You must," he said, "take the community just as it is, and make the best of it.   You wish to obtain its confidence; there is a short rule for doing this which you will find useful—deserve it. But, to deserve it in full measure you must unite many excellences, natural and acquired. As the basis of all the rest, you must have all those traits of character which fit you to enter into the most intimate and confidential relations with the families of which you are the privileged friend and counsellor. . . . By the oath of Hippocrates, the practitioner of ancient times bound himself to enter his patient's home with the sole purpose of doing him good, and so conduct himself as to avoid the very appearance of evil. Let the physician of today begin by coming up to this standard, and add to it all the more recently discovered virtues and graces. A certain amount of natural ability is requisite to make you a good physician, but by no means that disproportionate of some special faculty that goes by the name of genius." [6]

Of special value to the young practitioner were Dr. Holmes' words of advice to maintain good relations with one's fellow doctors. There have been seasoned physicians who might have profited by his suggestions. "The public," he declared, "is a very incompetent judge of your skill and knowledge, but it gives its confidence most readily to those who stand well with their professional brethren, whom they call upon when they or their families are sick, whom they choose to honorable offices, whose writings and teachings they hold in esteem. A man may be much valued by the profession and yet have defects which prevent his becoming a favorite practitioner, but no popularity can be depended on as permanent which is not sanctioned by the judgment of professional experts, and with these you will always stand on your substantial merits." [7]

And still further: "Your relations to your professional brethren may be a source of life long happiness and growth in knowledge and character, or they may make you wretched and end by leaving you isolated from those who should be your friends and counsellors. The life of a physician becomes ignoble when he suffers himself to feed on petty jealousies and sours his temper in perpetual quarrels. You will be liable to meet an uncomfortable man here and there in the profession,—one who is so fond of being in hot water that it is a wonder all the albumen in his body is not coagulated. There are common barrators among doctors as there are among lawyers,—stirrers up of strife under one pretext or another, but in reality because they like it. They are their own worst enemies and do themselves a mischief each time they assail their neighbors. . . . The great majority of the profession are peacefully inclined. Their pursuits are eminently humanizing, and they look with disgust on the personalities which intrude themselves into the placid domain of an art whose province is to heal and not to wound." [8]

To force home his advice, he declared: "If there happened to be among my audience any person who wished to know on what principles the patient should choose his physician, I should give him these few precepts to think over:

"Choose a man who is personally agreeable, for a daily visit from an intelligent, amiable, pleasant, sympathetic person will cost you no more than one from a sloven or a boor, and his presence will do more for you than any prescription the other will order.

"Let him be a man of recognized good sense in other matters, and the chance is that he will be sensible as a practitioner.

"Let him be a man who stands well with his professional brethren, whom they approve as honest, able, courteous.

"Let him be one whose patients are willing to die in his hands, not one whom they go to for trifles, and leave as soon as they are in danger, and who can say, therefore, that he never loses a patient." [9]

I had intended in this chapter to set forth a few general reflections of my own, based on great quantities of advice which I attempted to give the medical profession individually, and collectively, over many years. To place, however, my own thoughts alongside the sparkling words and sentences which I have quoted at such length, would seem almost an impertinence if not a sacrilege. I shall, therefore, now bring this book to a close, with the hope that it may be useful to the profession, but with the feeling that if it accomplishes no other purpose, it may reintroduce some of our present-day physicians to Oliver Wendell Holmes, whose words of inspiration to the practitioners of the healing art, deserve never to be forgotten.

ALPHABETICAL LIST OF CASES CITED

A

Albers v. Wilson
201 App. Div. (N. Y.) 775

Angulo v. Hallar
137 Md. 227

Antowill v. Friedmann
197 App. Div. (N. Y.) 230

Armstrong v. Bruce
4 Ontario Weekly Report 327

B

Baker v. Hancock
29 Ind. 456; 63 N. E. 323

Baker v. Wentworth
155 Mass. 338

Ballard v. Prescott
64 Me. 305

Barber's Estate
63 Ct. 393

Barburn v. Martin
62 Me. 536

Barrus v. Phaneuf
166 Mass. 123; 32 L. R. A. 619

Bauch v. Schultz
109 Misc. (N. Y.) 548

Beadle v. Paine
46 Or. 424

Becker v. Janinski
27 Abb. N. C. (N. Y.) 45

Behrman v. U. S.
258 U. S. 280

Bennan v. Parsonnet
83 N. J. L. 20

Benson v. Dean
232 N. Y. 52

Berkholz v. Benepe
153 Minn. 335

Birch v. Sees
178 App. Div. (N. Y.) 609

Blackburn v. Baker
227 App. Div. (N. Y.) 588

Blair v. Bartlett
75 N. Y. 150

Board of Comm'rs v. Lee
32 Pac. 841

Bodine v. Austin
156 Tenn. 353

Bohannon v. Bd. of Medical Examiners
24 Cal. App. 215

Boller v. Kinton
83 Col. 144

Bowers v. Santee
99 Ohio S. 361

Bradford v. People
20 Hun. (N. Y.) 309

Brown v. Bennett
157 Mich. 654

Brown v. Goffe
140 App. Div. (N. Y.) 353

Brown v. Travellers Ins. Co.
26 App. Div. (N. Y.) 544

AUTHORITIES AND ABBREVIATIONS USED

	Abbreviations
American Law Register, vol. 54	Am. Law Reg.
American Law Report	A. L. R.
American Law Review, vol. xxxiv	Am. Law Rev.
Bouvier Law Dictionary, Rawle's Third Edition, vol. iii	Bouvier
"What Medicine Can Do For Law" by Benjamin Cardozo (Bulletin New York Academy of Medicine, vol. v, 2nd Series, No. 7)	Cardozo
Chamberlayne's Modern Law of Evidence, vol. 5	Chamberlayne
Circuit Court of Appeals	C. C. A.
Civil Practice Act (New York)	Civ. Prac. Act
Corpus Juris	C. J.
Education Law (New York)	Educ. Law
"Anaesthesia" by James Tayloe Gwathmey, M. D. (Macmillan Co. 1925)	Gwathmey
Harvard Law Review	Har. Law Rev.
"Devils, Drugs and Doctors" by Dr. Howard W. Haggard (Harper Bros. 1929)	Haggard
"The Economic Contribution of Physicians to the Community" by Chas. Gordon Heyd, M. D.	Heyd
The Writings of Oliver Wendell Holmes (Medical Essays) vol. ix (Houghton Mifflin & Co.)	Holmes
"Foundations and Their Trends," by Samuel J. Kopetzky, M. D.	Kopetzky
Law Reports Annotated	L. R. A.
Legal Medicine & Toxicology, by Peterson, Haines & Webster, (2nd ed.) vol. I	L. M. & T.

New York State Bar Assocation, Report of, vol. xxxii	N. Y. S. Bar Assn.
New York State Journal of Medicine	N. Y. S. J. of M.
Penal Law, New York	N. Y. P. L.
Principles of Medical Ethics of American Medical Association	P. M. E.
Principles of Professional Conduct of Medical Society of the State of New York	P. P. C.
Regulations Treasury Department, Bureau of Prohibition	Reg. B. of P.
Ruling Case Law	R. C. L.
Chase Stephens' Digest on the Law of Evidence	Stephens
Thompson on Negligence	Thompson
Trevelyan's History of England	Trevelyan
"The Art of Cross Examination," by Francis Wellman (Macmillan Co. 1923)	Wellman
Wigmore on Evidence (Little, Brown & Co.)	Wigmore
Wharton on Evidence	Wharton

REFERENCES

INTRODUCTION

(1) Haggard pp. 99–102; Gwathmey, pp. 11–14; (2) Gwathmey p. 14; (3) Holmes pp. 349–50; (4) Haggard pp. 383–4; (5) Haggard pp. 381–2; (6) Cardozo p. 581; (7) Cardozo p. 589; (8) Cardozo pp. 593–4; (9) N. Y. J. of M. vol. 27, No. 12, June 15, 1927; (10) Kopetzky p. 10; (11) Kopetzky p. 10; (12) Holmes p. 417; (13) Cardozo p. 583; (14) quoted by Judge Cardozo in Harvard Law Rev. vol. xliv, No. 5, p. 683.

PART I—CHAPTER I

(1) N. Y. Educ. Law, sec. 1250; (2) Calif. Act of 1901 and Act of Mar. 4, 1907; Conn. sec. 2854, chap. 148, title 24, Laws of 1918; Ill. chap. 91, sec. 24, Laws of 1923; Mass. R. L. chap. 76, secs. 8, 9; Minn. chap. 188, sec. 4, 1927; N. J. P. L. 1894, chap. 458, p. 3332, Comp. Stat. of N. J.; Ohio, title 3, div. 2, chap. 20, sec. 1286, Page's Anno. Ohio Gen. Code; Pa. P. L. 639–649, sec. 1, Laws of 1911; (3) Dent v. West Virginia, 129 U. S. 114; (4) Commonwealth v. Zimmerman, 221 Mass. 185; (5) Bohannon v. Board of Medical Examiners, 24 Cal. App. 215, 229; (6) For N. Y. requirements see N. Y. Educ. Law secs. 1256–1260; (7) N. Y. Educ. Law, sec. 1263; (8) Peo. v. Ellis, 162 App. Div. 288; Peo. v. Mulford, 140 App. Div. 716, affd. 202 N. Y. 624; Peo. v. Alcutt, 117 App. Div. 546, affd. 189 N. Y. 517.

PART II—CHAPTER II

(1) Prin. of Med. Ethics of Amer. Med. Assn. chap. I, sec. 1; (2) id. chap. II, sec. 1; (3) id. chap. II, sec. 3; (4) Princ. of Prof. Con. of N. Y. M. S. sec. 3; (5) id. sec. 4; (6) N. Y. S. J. of M. vol. 26, No. 9, May 1, 1926; (7) Holmes p. 302.

CHAPTER III

(1) Pike v. Honsinger, 155 N. Y. 201; (2) Pike v. Honsinger, supra; (3) Pike v. Honsinger, supra; Carpenter v. Blake, 75 N. Y. 12; Link v. Sheldon, 136 N. Y. 1; Patten v. Wiggin, 51 Me. 594; Hitchcock v.

Burgett, 38 Mich. 501; Smothers v. Hanks, 34 Ia. 286; McCandless v. McWha, 22 Penn. St. 261; Becker v. Janinski, 27 Abb. N. C. 45; Winner v. Lathrop, 67 Hun. 511; Rowe v. Lent, 42 St. Rep. 483; Napier v. Greenzweig (U. S. Cir. Ct. of App. 2nd Cir.) 256 Fed. 196; Ewing v. Goode, 78 Fed. 442; Houghton v. Dixon, 29 Cal. App. 321; Landon v. Humphrey, 9 Conn. 209; Graiziger v. Hensler, 229 Ill. 365; McKee v. Allen, 94 Ill. App. 147; Carey v. Mercer, 239 Mass. 559; Chesley v. Durant, 243 Mass. 180; Angulo v. Hallar, 137 Md. 227; Lorenz v. Lerche, 157 Minn. 437; Berkholz v. Benepe, 153 Minn. 335; Bowers v. Santee, 99 Ohio S. 361; Stemmons v. Turner, 274 Penn. 228; Ely v. Wilbur, 49 N. J. 685; (4) Small v. Howard, 128 Mass. 131; (5) 48 C. J. 1116; (6) Baker v. Hancock, 29 Ind. 456, 63 N. E. 323; (7) Baker v. Hancock, supra; Rann v. Turtchell, 71 Atl. 1045 (Va.); Feeney v. Spalding, 89 Me. 111; Murdock v. Kimlerin, 23 Mo. App. 523; Wood v. Vroman, 215 Mich. 449; Hopkins v. Heller, 59 Cal. App. 447; Bouvier Law Dict. (Rawle's 3d Ed. vol. iii) p. 2587; (8) McCandless v. McWha, 22 Penn. St. 261; (9) L. M. & T. 2nd ed. 1923, vol. 1, p. 19.

CHAPTER IV

(1) Becker v. Janinski, 27 Abb. N. C. 45; (2) Carey v. Mercer, 239 Mass. 599; (3) id. p. 602; (4) McCandless v. McWha, 22 Penn. St. 261; Gentile v. DeVirgilis, 290 Penn. 50; (5) Jones v. Angell, 95 Ind. 376; Dashiell v. Griffith, 84 Md. 363; Gentile v. DeVirgilis, 290 Penn. 50; Williams v. Wundermann; 71 Wash. 390; (6) Carpenter v. Blake, 75 N. Y. 12; DuBois v. Decker, 130 N. Y. 325; Hibbard v. Thompson, 109 Mass. 286; Sanderson v. Holland, 39 Mo. App. 233; Richards v. Willard, 176 Pa. 181; Morris v. Despain, 104 Ill. App. 452; Chamberlain v. Morgan, 68 Pa. 168; Schultz v. Taske, 166 Wisc. 561; (7) Tish v. Welker, 5 Oh. St. C. P. 745; Beadle v. Paine, 46 Or. 424; Doyle v. Owen, 150 Ill. 415; 48 C. J. 1135.

CHAPTER V

(1) C. P. A. sec. 352; (2) Edington v. Mutual Life Ins. Co. 67 N. Y. 185, 194–5; (3) Griffiths v. Met. St. Ry. Co. 171 N. Y. 106; (4) Peo. v. Sliney, 137 N. Y. 570; Peo. v. Hoch, 150 N. Y. 291; (5) Kelly v. Dykes, 174 App. Div. 786; Meyer v. Knights of Pythias, 178 N. Y. 62; (6) Bauch v. Schultz, 109 Misc. 548; (7) Renihan v. Dennin, 103 N. Y. 573; (8) Meyer v. Knights of Pythias, 178 N. Y. 62; (9) Green v. Met. St. Ry. Co. 171 N. Y. 201; (10) Nelson v. Village of Oneida, 156 N. Y. 219; (11) Sparer v. Travelers Ins. Co. 185 App. Div. 861; (12) Heath v. Broadway & 7th Ave. R. Co. 57 N. Y. Sup. Ct. 496; (13) Burley v. Barnhard, 9 N. Y. St. Rep. 587;

(14) Estate of Darragh, 15 N. Y. St. Rep. 452; (15) Dillebar v. Home Life Ins. Co. 10 Wkly. Dig. 180; (16) Sloan v. N. Y. C. R. Co. 45 N. Y. 125; (17) Hunn v. Hunn, 1 Thomp. & C. 499; (18) Patten v. United Life & Accident Ins. Assn. 133 N. Y. 450; (19) Edington v. Mutual Life Ins. Co. 67 N. Y. 185, 196; (20) Weil v. Weil, 151 App. Div. 622; (21) Weil v. Weil, supra; Peo. v. Bloom, 193 N. Y. 1; (22) Hethier v. Jones, 233 N. Y. 370, 371-2; (23) Capron v. Douglass, 193 N. Y. 11, 15-17; Albers v. Wilson, 201 App. Div. 775; Fennelly v. Schenectady R. Co. 201 App. Div. 221; Dewey v. Cohoes & Lansingburgh Bridge Co. 170 App. Div. 117; McKenney v. Amer. Locomotive Co. 164 App. Div. 625; (24) Capron v. Douglass, supra, p. 17; (25) McKinney v. Grand St. etc. R. R. Co. 104 N. Y. 352, 355; (26) Mulligan v. Sinski, 156 App. Div. 35; (27) Capron v. Douglass, supra, p. 17; (28) Terier v. Dare, 146 App. Div. 375, 376; (29) Pierson v. Peo. 79 N. Y. 424, 434; (30) Peo. v. Brecht, 120 App. Div. 769; (31) Chamberlayne's Modern Law of Evidence, vol. 5, sec. 3701; (32) Wigmore on Evidence, Book 1, Part 3, Title 2, subtitle 3, chap. lxxxiv, sec. 1776; (33) MacEvitt v. Maass, 33 Misc., 552; affd. 64 App. Div. 382; 40 Cyc. 2390.

PART III—CHAPTER VI

(1) 48 C. J. 1112; (2) In re Rosenkrans, 84 N. J. Eq. 232; (3) 48 C. J. 1143-4; (4) Becker v. Janinski, 27 Abb. N. C. 45; (5) Volhell v. Wolf, (N. Y. App. Term, 1st Dept.) 151 N. Y. Supp. 918; (6) Pike v. Honsinger, 155 N. Y. 201; (7) id.; (8) id.; (9) McCandless v. McWha, 22 Penn. St. 261; (10) Pike v. Honsinger, supra; (11) Brown v. Goffe, 140 App. Div. 353; 48 C. J. 1143-4 and cases there cited; (12) Ewing v. Goode, 78 Fed. 442, 443; (13) Smith v. Dumont, 25 St. Rep. 382; (14) Smith v. Dumont, supra; (15) Pike v. Honsinger, supra; (16) Loudon v. Scott, 194 Pac. (Mont.) 488, 492; Houghton v. Dickson, 29 Cal. App. 321; State v. Housekeeper, 70 Md. 162; Stalock v. Holm, 100 Minn. 276; Spain v. Burch, 169 Mo. App. 94.

CHAPTER VII

(1) McGraw v. Kerr, 23 Cal. App. 163; (2) Houghton v. Dickson, 29 Cal. App. Rep. 321; Ewing v. Goode, 78 Fed. 442; Hall v. Steele, 193 Cal. 602; Robbins v. Nathan, 189 App. Div. 827; Lubbee v. Hilgert, 135 App. Div. 227, 231; Brown v. Goffe, 140 App. Div. 353; Lorenz v. Lerche, 157 Minn. 437; Funk v. Bonham, 151 N. E. 22; Moline v. Christie, 180 Ill. App. 334; Bennan v. Parsonnet, 83 N. J. L. 20; Delong v. Delaney, 206 Penn. 226; Carey v. Mercer, 239 Mass. 559; Angulo v. Hallar, 137 Md. 227; Caraway v. Graham, 218 Ala. 453; Patterson v. Marcus, 265 Cal. 222; Norhett v. Martin, 63 Col. 220; Slinak v. Foster, 106 Conn. 366; Phebus v. Mather, 181 Ill. App.

226 REFERENCES

274; Ramberg **v.** Morgan, 218 N. W. 492; Rainey v. Smith, 109 **Kan.**
692; Fenney **v.** Spalding, 89 Me. 111; Delahunt v. Finton, 244 Mich.
226; Loudon v. Scott, 58 Mont. 645; McDaniel v. Wolcott, 115 Neb.
675; VanEpp v. McKenry, 189 N. Y. S. 910; Hunter v. Burroughs,
123 Va. 113; Holton v. Burton, 222 N. W. 225; (3) Politics, vol. iii,
p. 11; (4) Pike v. Honsinger, 155 N. Y. 201; (5) Funk v. Bonham,
151 N. E. 22; (6) Sims v. Parker, 41 Ill. App. 284; (7) Lorenz **v.**
Lerche, 157 Minn. 437; (8) Delong v. Delaney, supra; (9) Moline **v.**
Christie, 180 Ill. App. 334; (10) Lubbee v. Hilgert, 135 App. Div.
227, 231; (11) Robbins v. Nathan, 189 App. Div. 827, 830; (12)
Ewing v. Goode, 78 Fed. 442, 443; (13) id.; (14) Ruback **v.**
McCleary, Wallin & Crouse, 220 N. Y. 188, 195; Yaggle v. Allen, 24
App. Div. 594; White v. Lehigh Valley R. R. Co. 220 N. Y. 131, 135;
Baudenbach v. Schwerdtfeger, 224 App. Div. 314; (15) Ewing **v.**
Goode, supra; (16) Pike v. Honsinger, supra.

CHAPTER VIII

(1) Evans v. Roberts, 172 Iowa 653; (2) id.; (3) Funk v. Bonham,
151 N. E. 22; (4) Benson v. Dean, 232 N. Y. 52; (5) id.; (6) id.;
(7) id.; (8) Mandelbaum v. Weil, 208 App. Div. 409; (9) Marke-
lonis v. Clark, 228 App. Div. 750; (10) Blackburn v. Baker, 227 App.
Div. 588. affd. 256 N. Y. Mem. 16; (11) Guell v. Tenney, 159 N.
R. 451; (12) Funk v. Bonham, supra; Wynne v. Harvey, 96 Wash.
397; Sims v. Parker, 41 Ill. App. 284; Cochran v. Gritman, 203
Pac. 289; (13) Antowill v. Friedmann, 197 App. Div. 230; (14) id.;
(15) Stemmons v. Turner, 274 Penn. 228; (16) id.; (17) Ewing v.
Goode, 78 Fed. 442; (18) Ewing v. Goode, supra; Hamilton v.
Harris, 204 S. W. 450; Runyan v. Goodum, 13 Am. L. Rep. 1403,
1413; 21 R. C. L. 386; (19) Sweeney v. Ewing, 35 App. Cas. 57,
affd. U. S. Sup. Ct. on a writ of error 228 U. S. 233; (20) Sweeney **v.**
Ewing, supra.

CHAPTER IX

(1) Hunner v. Stevenson, 122 Md. 40; (2) id.; (3) Reynolds **v.**
Smith, 148 Iowa 264; Harris v. Fall, 177 Fed. 79; 27 L. R. A. 1174,
100 C. C. A. 497; Baker v. Wentworth, 155 Mass. 338; Hitchcock **v.**
Burgett, 38 Mich. 501; Meyers v. Holborn, 58 N. J. L. 193; Morey **v.**
Thybro, 199 Fed. 760; Funk v. Bonham, 151 N. E. 22; Guell **v.**
Tenney, 159 N. R. 451; Blackburn v. Baker, 227 App. Div. 588; (4)
Perionowsky v. Friedman & ano. 4 Foster & F. 977, 980; Armstrong
v. Bruce, 4 Ont. Wkly. Rep. 327; (5) Harris v. Fall, 177 Fed. 79;
(6) Nelson v. Sandell, 202 Iowa 199; Robinson v. Crotwell, 175 Ala.
194; Jett v. Linoille, 202 Ky. 198, 259 S. W. 43; Morey v. Thybro,
supra; (7) Jett v. Linoille, supra; (8) Lawson v. Crane, 83 Vt. 115;

(9) Jett v. Linoille, supra; (10) Morey v. Thybro, supra; Keller v. Lewis, 65 Ark. 578; Hitchcock v. Burgett, 38 Mich. 501; Brown v. Bennett 157 Mich. 654; (11) Morey v. Thybro, supra; (12) id.; (13) Gould v. Kirlin, 192 Ill. App. 427; (14) Thompson on Neg. sec. 6723; (15) Keller v. Lewis, supra; Myers v. Holborn, 33 Atl. Rep. 389; Hitchcock v. Burgett, 38 Mich. 501; (16) Stokes v. Long, 159 Pac. 28; (17) Mullins v. Duvall, 258 Ga. 690; 14 S. E. 513; Myers v. Holborn, 58 N. J. L. 193; Langher v. Pointer, 5 Barn & C. 547; Milligan v. Wedge, 4 Perry & D. 714; DeForrest v. Wright, 2 Mich. 368; (18) Withington v. Jennings, 149 N. E. 201; (19) Brown v. Bennett, 157 Mich. 654; (20) Nelson v. Sandell, 202 Iowa 109; Mayer v. Hiphe, 183 Wisc. 382; (21) Boller v. Kinton, 83 Col. 144; (22) Stokes v. Long, 159 Pac. Rep. 28; Morey v. Thybro, 199 Fed. 760.

CHAPTER X

(1) Schloendorff v. New York Hospital, 211 N. Y. 125, 129; (2) Mohr v. Williams, 95 Minn. 261; (3) Moss v. Rishworth, 226 S. W. 215; Pratt v. Davis, 224 Ill. 300; Rolater v. Strain, 39 Okla. 572; (4) Moss v. Rishworth, supra; (5) Bennan v. Parsonnet, 83 N. J. L. 20; (6) Lurko v. Larny, 172 Mich. 122; (7) King v. Carney, 85 Okla. 62; (8) Hanson v. Reed, 21 Ohio W. P. N. S. 206.

CHAPTER XI

(1) Becker v. Janinski, 27 Abb. N. C. 45; Gerken v. Plimpton, 62 App. Div. 35; Potter v. Virgil, 67 Barb. 578; Gedney v. Kingsley, 15 N. Y. S. 675; (2) Ballard v. Prescott, 64 Me. 305; Williams v. Gillman, 71 Me. 21; Gerken v. Plimpton 70 N. Y. S. 793; Gillett v. Tucker, 67 Oh. St. 106; Murci v. Houghton, 89 Iowa 608; Barburn v. Martin, 62 Me. 536; (3) Becker v. Janinski, supra; (4) Tucker v. Gillett, 22 Ohio Cir. Ct. 664; (5) Gerken v. Plimpton, supra; Potter v. Virgil, 67 Barb. 580; (6) Barborn v. Martin, supra; (7) Lathrop v. Flood, 63 Pac. 1007; (8) Gedney v. Kingsley, 41 St. Rep. 794; (9) Kendall v. Brown, 74 Ill. 232; (10) Nelson v. Farrish, et al. 143 Minn. 368.

PART IV—CHAPTER XIII

(1) Blair v. Bartlett, 75 N. Y. 150; (2) 49 A. L. R. 553; (3) Jordahl v. Berry, 72 Minn. 192; Gobel v. Dillon, 86 Ind. 327; Leslie v. Mollica, 236 Mich. 610; Sale v. Eichberg, 105 Tenn. 333; Lawson v. Conaway, 37 W. Va. 159; (4) 48 C. J. 1133–4, cases cited in notes 90, 91, 92; (5) Rinando v. Weeks, 172 App. Div. 319; Goy v. Director General of Railroads, 191 App. Div. 680.

CHAPTER XIV

(1) Trevelyan's History of England, p. 125; (2) Buchanan v. Rou-
land, 5 N. J. L. 721; (3) Cray v. Hartford Fire Ins. Co. 6 F. Cases
No. 3375; 1 Blatchf. 580; (4) Riddlesbarger v. Hartford Fire Ins.
Co. 7 Wall. 386; (5) 37 C. J. 684–5; (6) Miller v. Calumet Lumber
Co. 121 Ill. App. 56, 66; (7) 37 C. J. 684.

CHAPTER XV

(1) Sec. 50, C. P. A.; (2) Sec. 48, C. P. A.; (3) Mass. Stat. 1921,
chap. 319; Minn. sec. 9193 Mason's Minn. Stats.; N. J. Rev. Stats.
1888, p. 594 as amended P. L. 1893; Penn. Act of 1855, P. L. 236, sec.
2; (4) Cal. sec. 340, subd. 3 of Code; Conn. sec. 6163 of Gen. Stats.;
Ohio sec. 11225, Throckmorton's Anno. Code of Ohio; (5) Md. Art.
57, sec. 1, p. 2052, Bagby Anno. Code of Md.; (6) Tulloch v. Haselo,
218 App. Div. 313; (7) Conklin v. Draper, 229 App. Div. 227, 229;
(8) Conklin v. Draper, 254 N. Y. 620; (9) Cappuci v. Barone, 165
N. E. 653; Fadden v. Satterlee, 43 Fed. 568; Coady v. Reins, 1 Mont.
424; Lattan v. Gillette, 95 Cal. 317; Hahn v. Claybrook, 100 Atl.
83; (10) 21 R. C. L. 401; (11) N. Y. Civ. Prac. Act., sec. 60;
Hyland v. N. Y. Central & H. R. R. Co., 24 App. Div. 417; 134
App. Div. 383.

CHAPTER XVI

(1) Harding v. Liberty Hospital Corp. 177 Cal. 520, 522; Marty v.
Somers, 35 Cal. App. 81; (2) Keirsey v. McNeemer, 197 Ill. App.
173; (3) Bodine v. Austin, 156 Tenn. 353; contra see Hickey v. Slat-
tery, 103 Conn. 716; (4) Horowitz v. Bogart, 218 App. Div. 158;
(5) Frankel v. Wolper, 181 App. Div. 485; Hurlburt v. Gillett, 96
Misc. 585, affd. 176 App. Div. 893; Monahan v. Devinny, 223 App.
Div. 547; (6) Mass. Stat. 1921, chap. 319; (7) Finch v. Bursheim,
122 Minn. 152; (8) Sec. 9193, Mason's Minn. Stats.

PART V—CHAPTER XVII

(1) Chase Stephens Digest p. 5; (2) id. p. 144; (3) Miller v. State,
9 Okla. Cr. 255; (4) Peo. v. Vanderhoff, 71 Mich. 158.

CHAPTER XVIII

(1) Miller v. State, 9 Okla. Cr. 255; (2) L. M. & T. vol. I, pp. 21–2;
(3) Wigmore, vol. I, sec. 562, subd. 2; (4) id. sec. 561; (5) Tullis v.
Kidd, 12 Ala. 648; (6) Voight v. In. Com. 297 Ill. 109, 130 N. E. 470;
(7) Maserjian v. Cadwell, 214 App. Div. 730; (8) id.; (9) Peo. v.

Rice, 159 N. Y. 400, 410; (10) Wigmore vol. I, sec. 561; Stephens art. 49, pp. 146–7; Slocovich v. Orient Ins. Co. 108 N. Y. 56; Stillwell etc. Co. v. Phelps, 130 U. S. 520; Struthers v. Philadelphia R. R. Co. 170 Pa. 291; Louisville & N. R. Co. v. Sandlin, 125 Ala. 585; Hunnicut v. Kirkpatrick, 39 Ark. 172; Nelson v. Sun Mutual Ins. Co. 71 N. Y. 454; Finn v. Cassidy, 165 N. Y. 584; Wigmore sec. 561; (11) Wigmore vol. I, sec. 569; (12) Author, N. Y. S. J. of M. Mar. 1, 1928, vol. 28, No. 5, p. 243; (13) Wigmore vol. I, sec. 563, subd. B; (14) N. Y. S. J. of M. vol. 28, No. 5, pp. 243, 252; (15) id.; (16) id. p. 253; (17) id. p. 253; (18) Wigmore vol. II, sec. 563, subd. 3; (19) Wigmore vol. I, sec. 563, subd. C; (20) Amer. Law Rev. vol. XXXIV, p. 1; (21) Report N. Y. S. Bar Assn. vol. XXXII, pp. 371–3; (22) Wellman p. 5.

CHAPTER XIX

(1) Stearns v. Field, 90 N. Y. 640; Jewett v. Brooks, 134 Mass. 505; Barber's Estate, 63 Ct. 393; Meeker v. Meeker, 74 Ia. 35; Hicks v. Citizens R. Co. 124 Mo. 115; (2) Lehman v. Knott, 196 Pac. 476, 479; (3) Rodgers, 2nd ed. sec. 28; (4) Lehman v. Knott, supra, p. 479; (5) id.; (6) Cochran v. Gritman, 203 Pac. 289; (7) id.; (8) Toy v. Mackintosh, 220 Mass. 430; (9) People v. Vanderhoff, 71 Mich. 176, 39 N. W. 28; (10) Wigmore vol. I, sec. 682, 2nd ed.; (11) Toy v. Mackintosh, supra; Louisville & Nashville R. Co. v. Falvey, 104 Ind. 409; Barber's Estate, supra; Crozier & M. St. R. R. Co. v. Ladies of the Macabees, 138 Minn. 16; Kearner v. Charles S. Tanner Co. 31 R. I. 203; (12) Wigmore vol. I, sec. 675; (13) Wigmore vol. I, sec. 683; (14) Wellman p. 95; (15) Wigmore sec. 686; (16) Wigmore sec. 686.

CHAPTER XX

(1) Egan v. Dry Dock & B. R. R. 12 App. Div. 556; (2) 22 C. J. 923, sec. 1127; (3) Amer. Law Reg. vol. 54, O. S. N. S. 45, p. 330, No. 6, June 1906; (4) Wigmore vol. 3, p. 2178, sec. 1692; (5) Foggett v. Fischer, 23 App. Div. 207; Wharton, sec. 666; Comm. v. Wilson, 1 Gray 337; Washburn v. Cuddihy, 8 Gray 430; People v. Millard, 53 Mich. 63; Epp v. State, 102 Md. 539; Harris v. Panama R. R. Co. 3 Bosw. 7; Matter of Mason, 60 Hun. 46; (6) Matter of Hock, 74 Misc. 15, 22; Foggett v. Fischer, supra; Pahl v. Troy City R. R. Co. 81 App. Div. 308; (7) id.; (8) Egan v. Dry Dock & B. R. R. supra.

CHAPTER XXI

(1) Peo. v. Raizen, 211 App. Div. 445, 461; (2) Birch v. Sees, 178 App. Div. 609, 610; (3) Tiffany v. Kellogg Iron Works, 59 Misc. 113,

114; (4) Tiffany v. Kellogg Iron Works, supra; Brown v. Travelers
Life & Acc. Ins. Co. 26 App. Div. 544; Peo. v. Montgomery, 13 Abb.
Pr. (N. S.) 207; (5) Matter of Schapiro, 144 App. Div. 1; (6) 2
A. L. R. 1377; (7) Ex Parte Dement, 53 Ala. 389; Ealy v. Shetler
Ice Cream Co. 150 S. E. 539; Sup. Ct. of App. W. V.; Schofield v.
Little, 58 S. E. 666, Ct. of App. Ga.; (8) Dixon v. People, 168 Ill.
179; Wright v. People, 112 Ill. 540; Board of Commissioners v. Lee,
32 Pac. 841, Ct. of App. Col.; Summers v. State, 5 Tex. 365; State v.
Teipner, 36 Minn. 535; Flinn v. Prairie County, 60 Ark. 204; (9)
Barrus v. Phaneuf, 166 Mass. 123, 32 L. R. A. 619; (10) Chamber-
layne vol. 3, sec. 2371; (11) Wigmore vol. 3, sec. 2203.

PART VI—CHAPTER XXIII

(1) Author, N. Y. S. J. of M. vol. 26, No. 21, Nov. 1, 1926.

PART VII—CHAPTER XXIV

(1) N. Y. Penal Law sec. 244.

CHAPTER XXV

(1) N. Y. Penal Law sec. 80; (2) Peo. v. Phelps, 133 N. Y. 267, 270;
(3) N. Y. Penal Law sec. 261; (4) N. Y. Penal Law sec. 2; (5) Peo. v.
Gardner, 144 N. Y. 119; (6) Peo. v. Moran, 123 N. Y. 265; (7) Peo.
v. Conrad, 102 App. Div. 566; (8) Bradford v. Peo. 20 Hun. 309;
Peo. v. Hammer, 194 N. Y. 712, 232 N. Y. 565; Fleming v. Peo. 27
N. Y. 329, Lamb v. State, 67 Md. 524; State v. Lee, 69 Ct. 186; (9)
Bradford v. Peo. supra; (10) Peo. v. Hammer, supra; (11) Sec. 317
Cal. Penal Code; (12) vol. 2, sec. 119, p. 1784 N. J. Comp. Stats.;
(13) Art. 27, sec. 3, p. 970 Md. Bagby Anno. Code; (14) Sec. 6200,
Title 56, chap. 327, Gen. Stat. of Conn.; (15) Chap. 272, sec. 19,
Gen. Laws; (16) Sec. 10175 Mason's Minn. Stat.; (17) Sec. 7662, p.
722 Digest Stat. Law of Pa.; (18) N. Y. Penal Law sec. 80; (19)
State v. Loomis & Blinn, 90 N. J. L. 216; (20) State v. Loomis, 89
N. J. L. 8; (21) Commonwealth v. Holles, 297 Ill. 399; Peo. v. Sea-
man, 107 Mich. 348; Commonwealth v. Blair, 126 Mass. 40; Peo. v.
Molineaux, 168 N. Y. 264; (22) Commonwealth v. Holles, supra;
(23) Report on Pa. Penal Code p. 722, Digest of Stat. Laws of Pa.;
State v. Owens, 22 Minn. 238; State v. Madden, 161 Minn. 132;
Smith v. State, 33 Me. 48; State v. Longstreth, 19 N. D. 268; Lamb v.
State, supra; State v. Gediche, 43 N. J. L. 91; (24) Geer v. State of
Ohio, 16 O. C. C. 142; (25) N. Y. Penal Law sec. 1050, subd. 2;
(26) N. Y. Penal Law sec. 1051; (27) Peo. v. McGonegal, 62 Hun.
622; 17 N. Y. S. 147; Peo. v. Hammer, 194 N. Y. 712; 232 N. Y. 565.

REFERENCES

CHAPTER XXVI

(1) Cal. Penal Code sec. 317; sec. 21, chap. 272 Gen. Laws of Mass.; sec. 10188 Mason's Minnesota Stat.; secs. 13033–4–5 Throckmorton's Anno. Code of Ohio; secs. 7663–4 Digest of Pa. Stat. Laws; (2) N. Y. Penal Law secs. 1141, 1142; (3) Peo. v. Byrne, 99 Misc. 1; Peo. v. Sanger, 222 N. Y. 192; (4) Peo. v. Byrne, supra; (5) Peo. v. Sanger, supra; (6) Peo. v. Sanger, supra.

CHAPTER XXVII

(1) Act of Dec. 17, 1914 amended by secs. 703, 704 of Revenue Act of 1926, Acts of Jan. 22, 1927 and Mar. 3, 1927; (2) id. sec. 9; (3) id. sec. 2 (a); (4) id. sec. 1; Art. 9 Regs. No. 5, Treasury Dept. Bur. of Pro. effective June 1, 1928; (5) id. sec. 8; (6) id. sec. 9; (7) id. sec. 8; (8) id. sec. 1; (9) Regs. art. 16; (10) Regs. art. 83; (11) Regs. art. 85; (12) Linder v. U. S. 268 U. S. 5; (13) Linder v. U. S. supra; (14) Simmons v. U. S. 300 Fed. 321; Behrman v. U. S., 258 U. S. 280; Hobart v. U. S. (C. C. A. 6th Cir.) 299 Fed. 784; (15) Regs. No. 35, art. 117; (16) Linder v. U. S. supra; (17) Linder v. U. S. supra; (18) Linder v. U. S. supra; (19) Linder v. U. S. supra; (20) Linder v. U. S. supra; (21) Regs. No. 5, art. 85; (22) Regs. No. 5, art. 85; (23) Regs. No. 5, art. 108; (24) N. Y. Penal Law sec. 1746.

CHAPTER XXVIII

(1) Nat. Pro. Act. Regs. No. 5, Jan. 1, 1928; (2) id. sec. 7, 41 Stat. 305; (3) Lambert v. Yellowley, 272 U. S. 581.

CHAPTER XXIX

(1) N. Y. Penal Law sec. 1052, subd. 3; (2) id. sec. 1053; (3) id. sec. 1760; (4) id. sec. 1937.

CHAPTER XXX

(1) N. Y. Penal Law sec. 1232.

CONCLUSION

(1) Haggard p. 75; (2) Holmes p. 377; (3) Holmes pp. 377–8; (4) Holmes p. 371; (5) Holmes p. 383; (6) Holmes pp. 383–4; (7) Holmes p. 385; (8) Holmes pp. 392–3; (9) Holmes pp. 390–1.

INDEX

A

Abandonment,
  dismissed by patient, 105
  sufficient notice to procure another surgeon, 105
  consultant no duty to continue, 109.
Abortion,
  as defined by New York Statute, 182
  intent necessary, 183
  not criminal if performed to preserve woman's life or child, 184
  burden on doctor to prove abortion not criminal, 184
  actual pregnancy not necessary, 184–185
  intent and overt act sufficient, 183
  intent to commit provable by circumstances, 185
  proof other abortions admissible to show intent, 185
  penalty for commission of, 182
  death resulting from illegal, (See Manslaughter).
Anaesthetist,
  responsibility of, for negligence of operating surgeon, 90.
Assault,
  (See Operations Without Consent).
Avoiding suit,
  suggestions on, 110–114.

C

Contraception,
  New York Statute, 187–188
  power of state to enact statute, 188

when physician may give advice, 189.
Contributory Negligence,
  failure to follow proper instructions, 23
  bar to suit against doctor, 119.
Cure,
  physician not guarantor, 16.

D

Doctors,
  nature of relationship to patient, 9
  degree of skill and care required by law, 15–22
  duty to use best judgment, 19
  keep abreast of times, 20
  follow approved methods in general use, 16
  relationship same even though receives no fee, 30
  not guarantor, 16
  instructions of, must be followed, 23
  incompetent to testify to confidential communications, (See Privileged Communications)
  actions against, for malpractice
  (See Negligence or Malpractice)
  responsibility of, for acts of nurses, internes, other doctors, 87–98
  responsibility of anaesthetist or onlooker for negligence of operating surgeon, 90
  responsibility of physician for substitute sent or recommended by him, 94
  (See Expert Testimony)

233

www.ingramcontent.com/pod-product-compliance
Lightning Source LLC
Chambersburg PA
CBHW021554210326
41599CB00010B/433